TAKE A WALK ON THE WILDE SIDE—FOR A SUPPLY OF SIDE-SPLITTING GAGS AND GUFFAWS!

It's the book that gives business the business, and gets right to the bottom line!

*How to out-gross the Gross National Product

*How to keep up with the Dow Joneses

*How to tell if Wall Street is bullish—or just plain bull!

IT'S WHOLESALE FUN AT BARGAIN BASEMENT PRICES!

YOU'LL LAUGH ALL THE WAY TO THE BANK!

THE OFFICIAL EXECUTIVES JOKE BOOK

Bantam Books by Larry Wilde
Ask your bookseller for the books you have missed.

The Official Sports Maniacs Joke Book
The *Absolutely Last* Official Sex Maniacs Joke Book
The Official Book of John Jokes
The Official Politicians Joke Book
The Official Rednecks Joke Book
The *Last* Official Smart Kids Joke Book
The *Absolutely Last* Official Polish Joke Book
The *Last* Official Irish Joke Book
The *Last* Official Sex Maniacs Joke Book
The Larry Wilde Book of Limericks
The Official Lawyers Joke Book
The Official Doctors Joke Book
More The Official Sex Maniacs Joke Book
The Last Official Jewish Joke Book

THE OFFICIAL EXECUTIVES JOKE BOOK

by Larry Wilde

Illustrations by Ron Wing

BANTAM BOOKS
TORONTO • NEW YORK • LONDON • SYDNEY • AUCKLAND

For Jef Blum—
The exec's exec

THE OFFICIAL EXECUTIVES JOKEBOOK
A Bantam Book / February 1986

ISBN 0-553-25422-7

Published simultaneously in the United States and Canada

Bantam Books are published by Bantam Books, Inc. Its trademark, consisting of the words "Bantam Books" and the portrayal of a rooster, is Registered in U.S. Patent and Trademark Office and in other countries. Marca Registrada. Bantam Books, Inc., 666 Fifth Avenue, New York, New York 10103.

PRINTED IN THE UNITED STATES OF AMERICA

O 0 9 8 7 6 5 4 3 2 1

Contents

Introduction

Ethnic humor continues to be the most popular form of put-down joke in America. But people still have the need to poke fun at politicians, priests, doctors, and lawyers, in fact, at any authority figure. Of course, all bosses come in for their share of ribbing along with business and corporate leaders. There is no other way to maintain sanity in the sanitarium.

Here's an example of the kind of humor Americans resort to when the need to mock the mighty corporate structure arises. It's tasteless. It's sick. It's . . .

After a poisonous gas leak had killed thousands in India, comics kidded: Here's the new "Union Carbide Song":

"Ten Little, Nine Little, Eight Little Indians . . ."

The sharpest deal in this country was the Dutch purchase of Manhattan from the Indians. Jokes about buying and selling have been flying ever since:

> Peter Minuit had just conned Manhattan Island out of the Carnarsie Tribe, and was standing with the sellers on the banks of the East River surveying the purchase. "Hold it!" he exclaimed. "Isn't that Brooklyn over there?"
>
> "Listen, wise guy," said the Carnarsie chief, "for $24 you expect the place to be perfect?"

Bartering in the marketplace is part of human nature. Everybody does it, whether it's an advertising exec, department-store buyer, company purchasing agent, housewife, or hooker.

> Strulowitz was leaving the blackjack table in Las Vegas when he spotted the most shapely, raven-haired woman he had ever seen. Talking to her at the bar, he discovered two

things: she was a full-blooded Indian, and her price was two hundred dollars!

"Two hundred dollars!" sputtered Strulowitz. "For God's sake, all of Manhattan only cost twenty-four!"

"That's right, honey," said the Indian maiden, "but Manhattan just lies there!"

Earning enough to purchase the creature comforts is very often the motivation for starting up a business venture. The executive giants of industry—Lee Iacocca, Richard J. Ferris, George Ball, William Simon—all started with small enterprises. Perhaps that is what motivated two Polish football players from a Michigan university to embark on a business venture for the summer.

Pavlik and Brakowski bought a truck load of watermelons. They paid one dollar each for them.

They sold every one of the melons for one dollar each. After counting up their money the Polacks realized they had the same amount they spent.

"See, you dummy!" exclaimed Pavlik. "I told you we should have got a bigger truck!"

There is wheeling and dealing between businessmen. The marketplace is filled with con men, flimflammers, swindlers, embezzlers, cheaters, and chiselers. How do you lampoon disreputable people like that? Like this:

Lubin and Kreps, two garment manufacturers, met on Seventh Avenue in New York.

"Good morning!" said Lubin.

"Don't talk to me," replied Kreps. "You're so crooked that the wool you've been pulling over my eyes is fifty percent polyester."

There are probably more Chinese and Arabic entrepreneurs than any other ethnic groups. Yet, in the West, commercial enterprise appears to be dominated by the Jewish people. Many of the successful business leaders are often quizzed by youngsters anxious to learn the secret of their accomplishments:

> Levine had made a fortune in the pants business.
>
> "How did you do it?" asked the college student going for his doctoral degree in business administration.
>
> "Very simple," explained the old man. "When I arrived in this country I went out and bought pants for one dollar and I sold them for two dollars. For me, the one-percent profit was enough."

The business world is just as vulnerable to parody and satire as any other social or cultural arena. When it comes to ridiculing rigid trade transactions or pricking the bubble of executive pomposity, nothing is sacred. The scathing scalpel of humor cuts arrogance to the bone.

> Gottlieb, a shopkeeper, waited at the entrance to the Pearly Gates while St. Peter spoke to Watkins, a Black who had also just died.
>
> "You can have anything you want," said St. Peter.
>
> "Ah'd like a million dollars."
>
> "Done!"
>
> Watkins was given the money and he walked happily away. Now St. Peter said to Gottlieb, "You will be granted any wish you make. What would you like?"
>
> "I'd like to have $20 worth of fake jewelry," said the old Jewish man, "and ten minutes alone with that Black fella!"

In the pages that follow you will find the funny side of butchers and bankers, plumbers and presidents—everybody you do business with. Here come the corporate clowns, the management magicians and the yuppie yahoos. They're all here—waiting on stage to give you some giggles and guffaws.

LARRY WILDE
Sea Ranch

Managerial Merriment

During the lunch break, the foreman saw one of his factory workers limping.

"What's hurting?" he asked.

"There's a splinter in my foot," replied the employee.

"Why don't you pull it out?"

"What, on my own time?"

* * *

The social worker, seeing a tramp lying in the sun, asked, "Why don't you get a job?"

"Why?"

"To have some money in the bank."

"Why?"

"So that when you get enough you could retire and stop working."

"I'm not working now."

* * *

Applicant: I like the job, but the last place paid more, and gave overtime bonuses, holidays with pay, and sabbaticals.

Employer: Why did you leave?

Applicant: The firm went broke.

* * *

Woodley sat before the personnel director. "If I take this job, will I get a raise every year?"

"Yes, if you do a good job."

"I knew there was a snag somewhere."

* * *

EXECUTIVES BALANCE SHEET

(Year Ending Dec. 31, 1985)

Population of the U.S.	240,000,000
Persons 60 and over	–40,000,000
Left to do the work	200,000,000
Persons under 21	–60,000,000
Gov't. workers and adult dependents	–40,000,000
Left to do the work	100,000,000
Armed service and adult dependents	–20,000,000
Left to do the work	80,000,000
State and local employees and adult dependents	–30,000,000
Left to do the work	50,000,000
Persons drawing federal and state benefits	–30,000,000
Left to do the work	20,000,000
Persons and dependents living on income	–10,000,000
Left to do the work	10,000,000
Persons in hospitals and jails; the insane and incapacitated	–9,500,000
Left to do the work	500,000
Religious and charity workers	–400,000
Left to do the work	100,000
Bums and others who won't work	–99,998
Left to do the work	2

Two—You and Me

And if you don't get your butt in gear I'll have to run this country by myself.

Did you ever notice that a man who makes good dough always ends up with the best cookies?

* * *

"Are you looking for work, young man?"

"No, but I'd like a well-paid job."

* * *

A Florida bank director asked the new clerk why the cashier had gone to the races during business hours.

"He told me it was his last chance to get the books to balance," said the clerk.

* * *

A bank personnel officer in Argentina wrote to a London bank for a reference on a job applicant named William Farnsworth. He wrote:

"I understand that Mr. Farnsworth was a tried and trusted employee of yours."

He received this reply:

"Mr. Farnsworth, I'm sorry to say, was trusted, and he will be tried if he ever has the temerity to return to Britain."

* * *

At closing time in a Nashville bank, fifty $1,000 bills were missing. The tellers worked all night to find them, but in vain. Ida Mae reported for work the next morning and learned what happened. "Oh, it's all right," she said, "Ah took them home to show mah family the kind of work ah'm doin'."

* * *

Boss: You should have been here at 8:30.
Employee: Why, did anything unusual happen?

* * *

NOTICE TO ALL EMPLOYEES

Some time between starting and quitting time, without infringing on lunch period, coffee breaks, rest periods, storytelling, ticket-selling, holiday planning, and the recapping of yesterday's TV programs, we ask that each employee try to find some time for a work break.

This may seem radical, but it may aid steady employment and assure regular pay checks.

* * *

Jan and Michel Rosen, the elegant Santa Rosa restauranteurs, regale customers with this rib tickler:

A German Shepherd was out looking for a job. He passed an office with a sign that said:

WANTED
Experienced Worker who is excellent typist, can operate computer, and is bilingual.

"That's for me," thought the dog. He picked up the sign and walked into the office.

The astonished manager said, "Don't tell me you're applying for the job?"

"Woof," said the German Shepherd, and he walked over to the typewriter and typed 75 words a minute without an error. Then he went to the computer and produced a perfect readout on the history of dog breeding.

"Well, that's great," said the manager, "but are you bilingual?"

"Meow! Meow!" said the dog.

A college graduate was having a tough time making the grade in a brokerage house.

"Tell me," implored a partner in desperation, "why did your Uncle Thornton send you down here?"

"Well," the graduate explained, "he says he wants to get square with Wall Street for what happened to him in 1929."

* * *

Barton, a young technician on duty in the master control room of a gigantic electric-power complex, was asked to demonstrate the operation to a group being shown through the plant. The visitor's host was the president of the company.

Barton deftly threw switches, pressed buttons, and turned dials. Computer tapes whirled, lights flashed, electric arcs cracked across the room, and smoke poured out of the infernal apparatus. Then all was quiet. The machine died. The engineer had wrecked the panel that controlled electric power to almost half of the U.S.A.

"Well Barton!" barked the embarrassed and furious company president. "Now what are you going to do?"

"I'm going to buy a small farm in Kansas, sir."

* * *

OVERHEARD ON A JET TO NEW YORK

Stewardess: I'm sorry, Mr. Metcalf, but we left your wife behind in Chicago.
Corporate Exec: Thank goodness! I thought I was going deaf.

* * *

When a man's really keen on hard work, the odds are that he's an employer.

* * *

A stockbroker was forced by illness to take time off from his business. In the hospital, the nurse had just taken his temperature.

"What is it now, nurse?" he asked.

"102," she replied.

"When it goes to 102 and a half—sell," said the broker.

* * *

Who are the world's most desirable consumers?

A Black with a welfare check.

A Polack with a credit card.

A Jew who's cheating on his wife.

* * *

George Sam George, the magnificent Maxell tape sales director, loves this spirit-lifter:

When Dooley died, his body was frozen as indicated in his will. Fifty years later he was defrosted and he immediately phoned his brokerage. "What's the stock market done the past 50 years?" he asked.

With the aid of a computer, a broker soon was able to report that his 100 shares of IBM were now worth ten million, his 100 shares of General Motors worth eight million, and his oil holdings had increased to twenty-two million.

"Great!" exclaimed Dooley. "I'm rich!"

At which point the telephone operator interrupted and said, "Your three minutes are up, sir. Would you please deposit five million dollars?"

* * *

The only difference between the current stock market and the Titanic is that the Titanic had a band.

* * *

MONOLOGUE

A conversation between a real estate promoter and a prospect.

* * *

Melby, the black sheep of the family, returned to his New Hampshire home after years of adventuring in the West. One night he admitted to his father that he'd once bought a silver mine in Colorado for $1,000—all the money he could beg or borrow.

"Well," he finished, "the mine was an outright phoney."

"I knew they'd rope you in," crowed the old man. "You'd just be stupid enough to buy into a phoney mine!"

"I didn't lose anything by it, though," continued the son. "I just formed a company and sold half the stock to some New Hampshire man for $10,000."

"My God," murmured the old man, "I'll bet I'm the one who bought it."

* * *

Arnold Constable, who amassed millions on the stock market, fell gravely ill.

"Anna," he said to his granddaughter, "I'm afraid my time has come. I'm dying."

"Hush," whispered Anna soothingly. "With your constitution you'll live to be a hundred and twenty."

"That's foolish thinking," retorted the old stockbroker. "Why should God wait till I go all the way up to a hundred and twenty when he can get me at only seventy-nine?"

* * *

Flipping through her morning newspaper, Mrs. Berkowitz was attracted by a headline in the financial section. She read it with mounting perplexity, then turned to her husband and said, "What makes the market go up and down?"

"Oh, all kinds of things," he replied. "Commodity fluctuations. Inflationary pressures. International imbalances. Political tensions. Financial instability."

She put down the paper and said, "Look, if you don't know, why don't you just say so?"

* * *

Milt Josefsberg, the veteran Hollywood comedy writer has invested part of his income over the years in the stock market. He admits that besides writing funny lines he spends "a great deal of time keeping up with the Dow Joneses."

* * *

A Hollywood business manager was just caught absconding with his client's securities because he had made the fatal error of putting back too much. He got a stiff sentence for being generous to a vault.

* * *

Walsh and Tofler met in a Yuppie wine bar. "I've got a hot tip for you," announced Walsh.

"Really?"

"Sell your Beatrice stock."

"Good heavens, why?" asked Tofler.

"I heard they just bought Trojan and Haagen-Daz and they're going to make a condom that melts in your mouth."

* * *

While skiing at Vail, Colorado, Weldon, a Yuppie computer exec, phoned his stockbroker and bought 10 shares of stock at 10¢ a share. The next day it went up to $1.10. He phoned his broker and said, "Buy me a hundred shares!"

The next day the stock went up to $2 and Weldon ordered a 1000 shares.

Two days later the stock climbed to $5 a share. "Buy me 5000 shares," said Weldon.

The next day the stock went all the way up to $10 a share. Weldon called his broker and said, "Sell!"

The broker said, "To whom?"

* * *

INDIAN REAL ESTATE BROKERS

Escrows

* * *

Elizabeth Feldman, the rosy Redwood Podiatric Clinic administrator, plies patients with this cheery chuckle:

A Hawaiian real estate salesman was showing Henderson some property near Honolulu and was pulling out all the stops. He finished up with, "Why, the climate's the best in the world. Do you know, no one ever dies here?"

Just then, a funeral procession came into view and wound slowly down the street. The real estate agent removed his hat and said, "Poor old undertaker. Starved to death."

FUNERAL HOME
INQUIRE
FOR SALE
HATS OFF REALTY

A Georgetown University physics professor turned to his graduate class and said, "I defy you to name anything faster than the speed of light."

"That's easy," barked a student. "A yuppie in a BMW on his way to a Rolex watch sale."

* * *

"This house," said the real estate salesman, "has both its good points and its bad points. To show you I'm honest, I'm going to tell you about both. The disadvantages are that there is a chemical plant one block south and a slaughterhouse a block north. There's a glue factory on the east and a rubber factory a few blocks west of here!"

"What are the advantages?" inquired the prospective buyer.

"The advantage is that the price is low and you can always tell which way the wind is blowing."

* * *

"Would you like to see our model home?" asked the real estate broker.

"I sure would!" the prospective customer eagerly responded. "What time does she quit work?"

* * *

Don Jacobs, the award-winning California architect, regales satisfied clients with this rib buster:

The Lenharts decided to move out to the suburbs. She had lots of free time to look for a new house, so she signed up with a real estate agent.

Mrs. Lenhart spent several weeks looking at houses but found something wrong with each one. She never liked even one house well enough to have her husband look at it with her.

Finally, the salesman grew impatient. "Madam, why do you need a home?" he exploded. "You were born in a hospital, educated in a school building, courted in an automobile, and married in a church. You live at hamburger stands and eat out of freezers and cans. You spend your mornings at the golf course, your afternoons at the bridge table, and your evenings at the movies. All you really need is a garage!"

* * *

BROKER'S SERENADE

She was only a real estate salesman's wife but she gave lots away.

* * *

Slayton, a Cleveland real estate broker, was showing the dilapidated house to a prospective buyer. It looked like one blow would make it collapse like an accordian.

"You can do a lot with this place," he said.

"Sure," said the nonbuyer, "if you're handy with money."

* * *

Val Sabuco, the ingenious investment advisor, cracks up clients with this cutie:

Anderson, a big Chicago wheeler-dealer, owned a loft building, a marble yard with dock privileges, a factory site, and a summer garden. He proposed to swap all this with Bilby who owned three condominiums, a small subdivision, an abandoned lime kiln, and a farm.

"He assumes an $80,000 mortgage on the loft building," explained Anderson to his wife, "and I take over a second mortgage on the subdivision. Get me?"

"I guess so," responded the wife, "but if you've got all the details so cleverly worked out, what's holding up the deal?"

"I sign nothing," he declared, "till he gives me ten dollars in cash!"

* * *

The real estate broker was showing a model house to a newly married couple. "This is the hobby room," the agent explained as they entered one room. "Do you have a hobby?"

"Oh, yes," said the husband.

"And what is it?" asked the agent.

"Looking at model homes," was the reply.

* * *

Osgood bought a house near a river bank, despite the fact that the cellar seemed rather damp. "Snug as a bug in a rug," assured the salesman. "This cellar is dryer than the Sahara Desert."

A month later Osgood charged into the real estate office, prepared to wring the salesman's neck. "You and your Sahara," he cried. "I put two mousetraps in that cellar, and when I went down to look at them this morning they had caught a flounder and a haddock!"

* * *

Why are real estate brokers the naughtiest people on earth?

Just tell them what place you like and they'll offer to show it to you.

* * *

Loman, the salesman, banged on the door and got no reply. Desperate for a sale, he knocked again. Finally the door opened and there stood a frumpy young woman, half asleep, neckline open, smudged makeup over her face, hair straggling down her shoulders, and a cigarette drooping from the corner of her mouth. ''Hey,'' she said, ''what's all the noise about?''

''I'm selling sets of books, ma'm, and I'd like you to have a look at a sample because your children need to be better educated these days,'' declared Loman.

''Imagine waking me up like that first thing in the damn morning!'' snorted the woman. ''What kind of nut are you? In the first place I don't have no kids, in fact, I ain't married, and secondly I can't stand around in the nude listening to your stupid sales pitch. Anyway, what the hell do I want with encyclopedias? I'm the principal of a private girls' school and . . . shit, now I'm going to be late for the damn morning prayers!''

Finkelman, the renting agent in a brand-new luxury apartment house on the East Side, was pointing out the various features of an apartment. The prospective tenant, Mr. Foreman, agreed that the apartment was attractive but he hesitated, ". . . because the building seems flimsily constructed, and not too steady."

"What do you expect?" snapped Finkelman. "The wallpaper isn't up yet!"

* * *

Boss: Why do you want a raise?

Worker: Sir, I wouldn't ask but my kids have been at me ever since they found that other families eat three times a day.

* * *

A little boy was standing on the corner of a Detroit street yelling, "I'm selling my apple for a Greyhound bus. I'm selling my apple for a Greyhound bus!"

A man approached him and asked him why he was selling his apple for a Greyhound bus. The kid said, "If my sister can sell her cherry for a Cadillac I want to sell my apple for a Greyhound bus."

* * *

Hart was working in a lingerie shop when a woman of about 400 pounds walked in and said, "Young man, I'd like to see a girdle to fit me!"

He said, "So would I!"

* * *

Employer: Where have you been?
Laborer: Having a haircut.
Employer: You can't have your haircut on my time.
Laborer: Why not? It grew on your time!

* * *

Times may change but Southern hospitality will always remain.

A Tennessee factory owner who produced ladies blouses for a New York Company had the young president stay in his beautiful colonial home. One night the Tennesseean found his daughter making love to their northern guest on the hallway floor.

"Cora Mae!" he shouted. "Where is yo' Southern hospitality? Arch yo' back and get the gen'man's balls up off that cold marble flo'!"

* * *

Several Madison Avenue Yuppie ad execs were sipping Chardonnay at an East Side bar and discussing their troubles.

Hard luck Sibley topped them all when he dejectedly explained, "I've got a wife, a secretary, and a note from the bank—all overdue."

* * *

Jenkins and Cooper met on a Harlem street corner. "How you been, baby?" greeted Jenkins. "Ain't seen you around in years. Wha'choo now?"

"I'm a doctor, now," replied Cooper.

"No sheet! Wha'choo know 'bout doctorin'?"

"I knows everything."

"Wha'choo know 'bout venereal disease?"

"You talkin' to the venereal disease specialist. I was the Southern distributor for years."

* * *

"Wha'choo doin' Altois?"

"I'm gonna learn me a trade so I can tell the Welfare people what kind of work I'm out of."

* * *

Mr. Johnson walked into the Internal Revenue office to discuss his tax return. Another man behind the desk said, "What is your name?"

"Rufus Rastus Johnson!"

"That's impossible," retorted the government man. "My name is Rufus Rastus Johnson. How do you spell it?"

The taxpayer picked up a pencil and wrote, "X X X."

"That's the same way I spell mine," announced the tax collector. "But after that I put . . ." And he added, "X X X."

"What does that mean?"

"C.P.A."

* * *

Kendrick was walking up and down in front of a building in Harlem. A police car pulled up and one of the cops asked him why he was loitering.

"Ah'm waitin' for my wife," replied the Black. "She works in dat buildin' over there!"

"You mean to say your wife is a prostitute?" asked the astonished cop.

"No, suh," said Kendrick. "She ain't no prostitute. She only work one day a week. She's jus' a substitute!"

* * *

Crawford passed a tavern that had a sign in the window:

We Serve WHITES Only.

He entered the saloon anyway, sat at the bar, and ordered a whiskey. The bartender rushed to the rear of the tavern and reminded the boss of the "*We Serve WHITES Only*" sign.

"Never mind," said the owner. "Serve him his drink but charge him twenty bucks for it!"

Ten minutes later, Crawford ordered another whiskey. Again the bartender approached his employer, who said, "Okay, give it to him, but charge him fifty dollars!"

Soon Crawford ordered another drink. This time the boss said to the barkeep, "Charge him a hundred dollars a shot!"

As the bartender started to leave the owner added, "And change that sign in the window to '*We Serve BLACKS Only*'."

JOE'S BAR
WE SERVE WHITES ONLY
WE SERVE BLACKS ONLY

General Motors is coming out with a new special economy-size compact Cadillac. It's for Blacks on welfare.

* * *

Winslow was strolling along the beach one afternoon when he discovered a bottle lying in the sand. The Black boy picked it up and pulled out the cork. Suddenly, a gust of wind whooshed from the bottle and a genie appeared.

"You have released me from my prison," said the genie. "I will grant you two wishes."

"Hey, man," said Winslow, "ain't you supposed to be givin' folks three wishes?"

"Never mind that—you have two. What is your first wish?"

"Well, natchurly, I wants to be white."

The genie snapped his fingers and in a second the Black boy was white.

"And for your second wish?" asked the genie.

"Ah, I guess, what I wants, is to never have to work."

The genie snapped his fingers and in a second Winslow was Black again.

* * *

George walked into a swanky bar on Woodward Avenue in the Motor City and ordered a bottle of beer. He handed the Black bartender a dollar bill and was shocked to receive ninety cents change. "Isn't there some mistake?" asked George.

"No," said the barkeep. "A dime is all I'm charging you.

Twenty minutes later, George ordered a ham and cheese on rye. "That'll be fifteen cents!" said the barman.

"I can't understand it!" George exclaimed. "How can you sell this stuff so cheap?"

"Look, buddy, I just work here!" said the Black man. "The boss is upstairs with my wife. And what he's doin' to my wife, I'm doin' to his business!"

Salesman Snickers

The salesman finally got through to the big-shot businessman on the phone.

"Mr. Kramer, I've been trying to set up an appointment with you for a month."

"You'll have to make a date with my secretary," snapped the tycoon.

"I've already done that," said the salesman, "and we had a hell of a time, but I'd still like to see you."

* * *

Boss: What's this big item on your expense account?

Salesman: That's my hotel bill.

Boss: See that you don't buy any more hotels.

* * *

Neiman and Melnick, two New York shoe salesmen, were sent to Africa to open up new markets.

On the first day of their arrival in Zululand, Neiman sent a cable to the home office:

RETURNING ON NEXT PLANE.
IMPOSSIBLE SELL SHOES HERE.
EVERYBODY GOES BAREFOOT.

Two weeks later the sales manager finally received a cable from Melnick:

PILING UP ORDERS BY THE BUSHEL.
PROSPECTS UNLIMITED.
NOBODY HERE HAS SHOES.

* * *

Lolo Westrich, the irresistible Redwood Writers' Club exec, revels in this whimsical winner:

Morrison was ushered into a powerful tycoon's private sanctum at the end of a hectic day. "It speaks well for your power of persuasion that you've wangled your way in," said the mogul. "Fourteen other salesmen were booted out of here today."

"I know," said Morrison. "I'm all of them."

* * *

Related Sale was the subject of a pep talk given by Morton the manager of a huge drugstore. "For instance, if a customer wants razor blades," he told employees, "ask him how he's fixed for shaving cream and after-shave lotion. That way you can turn a small sale into a bigger one and earn a larger commission."

Link, the new clerk, was so impressed by the talk he tried the technique on his next customer, an embarrassed man who requested a box of Kotex for his wife. Ten minutes later, the store manager was amazed to see the customer staggering out loaded down with assorted fishing equipment, tackle, nets, boots, and a one-man inflatable life raft. "What happened?!" gasped the manager.

"*Related Sale,*" said the clerk.

"*Related Sale!*" exclaimed Morton. "But all he wanted was a box of—"

"I know, so I said, 'Look, mister, there isn't going to be much doing around your house this weekend. Why don't you take a fishing trip?' "

* * *

She was 'honey chil' in New Orleans,
The hottest of the bunch;
But on the old expense account,
She was gas, repairs, and lunch.

* * *

Robert Imbs, the magnetic Faber Castel Marketing Services Manager, makes merry with this whopper:

Anderson, a fanatical duck hunter rented a dog at a lodge and had wonderful luck with him. A month later he went back and described the dog he wanted because he had forgotten to ask its name.

"Oh, you want *Salesman*," beamed Drake the lodge owner. "We've raised his rate from $10 to $20."

Anderson took the dog out anyway and enjoyed another fine day. When he went back the following month, he asked for *Salesman*. Drake explained that the dog was now called *Super Salesman* and cost $50. Anderson took him out anyway, insisting he was well worth the money.

The next month when Anderson drove up in his car, the lodge owner said, "Sorry, you can't have your favorite dog this time."

"Why not?" asked the sportsman.

"A few days ago we made the mistake of naming him *Sales Manager*. Now, all he'll do is sit on his tail and bark."

SAL
MANAGER

Morgan was complaining to a friend. "At least," he grumbled, "I can say I'm the most independent salesman in the business."

"What do you mean?" asked the friend.

"I take orders from nobody!"

* * *

Whispered one pretty secretary to another, "That new sales manager may be married, but his right eye isn't!"

* * *

Bostwick the sales manager had his crew together lecturing them on how they should give their all for the firm. He ranted and raved for some time when he noticed that Morley in the front row kept sneezing. The more Bostwick talked the more Morley sneezed. Finally it got so bad the sales manager stopped.

"Hey," he said, "you seem to be getting a bad cold. I suggest that you leave."

"No," answered Morley. "I'm not getting a cold."

"What's wrong then?" demanded the manager.

"Oh," was the reply, "I'm allergic to horseshit!"

* * *

Donatelli smiled at the sexy suburban housewife and said, "No, I'm not selling brushes, and that's not my foot in the door!"

* * *

Belford wangled an interview with a tough, hard-to-sell sales manager. He walked into the prospect's office and muttered, "I don't suppose you want any life insurance, do you?"

"I certainly don't," screamed the sales manager. As Belford, head bowed, started toward the door, the manager said, "Come back here a minute, young fellow. It's my job to train salesmen at this plant, and I want to tell you I've never seen a worse salesman than you are."

Belford came back and listened to a one-hour lecture on the art of salesmanship. By the time he'd finished, the sales manager had worked himself up to such a pitch that he signed an order for a $25,000 policy. He handed it to the salesman and said, "Remember. The first thing to do is to learn a couple of standard, organized approaches."

"I've done that," said Belford. "I've got an approach for every type of prospect. What you've just seen was my standard approach for tough sales managers."

* * *

Simmons was summoned to the office to discuss his oversized expense account.

"How in the world," asked the manager, "do you manage to spend $100 a day for food?"

"It isn't hard," snapped the salesman. "I skip breakfast."

* * *

There's no man with more endurance
Than the man who sells insurance.

* * *

Oscar and Murray were rapping during a coffee break. "I can't figure it," sighed Oscar. "That new model sure turned on and I thought I really put it to her. But then afterward, she began asking why I hadn't managed to hold back just a little longer."

"Ah, well," reasoned Murray, "that's the way the nookie grumbles."

* * *

SALESMANSHIP

Making your wife feel sorry for the chick who lost her bra in your car.

* * *

Tobias, a publisher's rep, was passing a large pumpkin field when he felt nature's call.

He stopped his car and found a large pumpkin. Tobias took out his knife, cut the top out of the pumpkin, hollowed it out a bit, and sat down. When he was through, he put the lid back and went on his way.

As the book rep drove along and thought about it, he became ashamed of the dirty trick he had played on the farmer. As the weeks went by he felt more guilty. The next time he was in the vicinity, he decided to make amends.

Tobias stopped at the farmhouse and asked the farmer if he owned the field that had contained the pumpkins.

"Yep!" said the farmer.

The salesman explained what he had done, apologized, and offered to pay damages.

The farmer walked over to the phone, cranked it several times, and said, "Hello, Hi, this is Si. You were right about the pie!"

* * *

"Is Manny a good salesman?"

"Good? He could sell sand to Saudi Arabia."

* * *

Cora, the new girl in the office, landed a dinner invitation from the handsome sales manager. "Do you have a particular hobby?" he asked her over liqueurs in the restaurant.

"Yes," she replied. "I grow mushrooms in the basement of the apartment house where I live alone."

"Mushrooms? That's a strange interest. Why?"

"Well," said the girl, "I'm fascinated by things that grow in the dark."

* * *

The census taker was busy filling out his forms. "And what is your occupation?" he asked Rizzuto.

"I'm a pimp," was the answer.

"My God!" said the census man. "I can't put that down. Can't you think of something else to call it?"

"Well," said Rizzuto, "you might say I'm a crack salesman."

* * *

Did you hear about the shoe salesman with a lisp who got slapped when he asked a female customer to sit down while he "looked up her thize?"

* * *

Traveling through a small Southern town, Weiner stopped at the local grocery store for a cold drink. A field worker in torn overalls sat on a board across the pickle barrel, singing and playing a guitar. Weiner noticed that the man's testicles were hanging through a hole in his overalls into the opening of the barrel. He slipped up beside the farmer and whispered, "Do you know your balls are hanging in the pickles?"

"No," said the singer, "but you hum it and I'll strum it!"

* * *

During the hotel-room shortage, Ostrow was given a room with two beds and told that they would have to rent the other bed to someone else. He was in bed reading when the other occupant, Shirley, was shown in. Shirley was a beautiful blonde.

She glanced at Ostrow and started slowly to undress, exposing everything to her best advantage. When she was finally nude, Shirley posed for some time in front of the mirror first this way and then that. Finally she got in bed and, leaning over as near as she could, whispered, "How would you like to come in my bed?"

"No, thanks," croaked Ostrow. "I've already come in mine!"

* * *

Benny Friedman, California's hardware king, tells this jolly tall tale:

Greenberg believed he was the world's greatest salesman. He bragged to a friend that he could sell anything to anybody at anytime. To prove his boast, he left for Alaska with a shipment of electric fans. He went from igloo to igloo trying to sell them, and at each place he met the same reaction.

"Fan?" asked an Eskimo. "What the hell do we need a fan for? It's 60° below zero here now."

"Sure," replied Greenberg. "But you never can tell—tomorrow it could jump to zero."

IMPOTENCE

A total lack of response-ability.

* * *

Willard was playing a golf course for the first time and lost his bearings. On the eighth fairway he saw Phyllis a short way off and told her of his predicament.

"You're on the eighth and I'm on the ninth, just one hole ahead of you," she told him.

He continued playing and a little later became lost again. He spotted Phyllis and asked for more help.

"You're on the sixteenth," she said, "and I'm on the seventeenth, just one hole ahead of you."

After a shower in the clubhouse, Willard decided to have dinner there. When he entered the dining room, he saw Phyllis at a table by herself. He asked if he could share her table and she agreed. He inquired if she lived in the city and was told that she traveled, a saleslady.

"So do I," he replied. "What's your line?"

"I never say," she answered. "When I do, people laugh."

"I won't laugh," he promised. "What do you sell?"

"I sell Kotex," she said.

He burst out laughing.

"There," she said, "I told you you would laugh about what I sell."

"I'm not laughing about your product," he told her, "but about this afternoon. You're still one hole ahead of me. I sell toilet paper!"

* * *

Novack, the door-to-door major appliance salesman was fast-talking the luscious young housewife. "Besides, ma'am, I can arrange easy credit terms."

"How easy?"

"Nothing down but your panties!"

* * *

The traveling salesman on his way home for the weekend decided to stop at a farmhouse and buy some fresh chickens for Sunday dinner. The farmer wasn't home, but he finally persuaded the farmer's wife to sell him two good-sized hens for a dollar. That evening when she told her husband what had happened, he screamed, "Two chickens for a dollar! Woman, he screwed you!"

"Yes, but only because I fell while we were chasing them."

* * *

* * *

Young Crandall was driving along a country road on his way to a Louisville sales meeting when a bee flew into the car. Somehow the thing got down in his pants and stung him on his manhood. Howling with pain he managed to stop the car, jumped out, and rushed up to a nearby farmhouse where he banged on the door.

Clarabelle, the farmer's pretty daughter, came to the door and quickly brought him the glass of buttermilk he asked for. Throwing aside all reserve, for the pain was so great, Crandall whipped out his manhood and dunked it in the glass of buttermilk.

Clarabelle's eyes got big and her mouth fell open. Finally she said, "Yew know, Ah've always wondered how they refilled those things."

* * *

De Sapio had to be on the road quite a bit. Once before leaving town, to test his wife's virtue, he placed a bowl of cream under their bed with a little weight suspended from a cord, almost touching the cream. When De Sapio returned home two nights later the cream was churned to butter.

* * *

A traveling salesman picked up a good-looking farm girl who was walking along a Georgia highway. He drove for a while and then said, "Boy, you sure have pretty bosoms. "I'd give ten dollars just to feel 'em."

She said okay.

A little later he said, "You sure have gorgeous legs. I'd give twenty dollars just to feel them."

She said okay, so he felt them. Then he said, "I just can't stand it, I've got to have some. How much will you charge me?"

"Most of the boys give me four bits," she replied.

* * *

TRAVELING MAN'S TOAST

Here's to the kisses you've
snatched and vice versa.

* * *

"I just got an order for thirty thousand dollars," crowed Carlson to another salesman.

"You're a liar," retorted the other.

"I am not!" insisted Carlson. "Here's the cancellation to prove it."

* * *

Farmer Chadwell was busy working in the north forty when his little son, Boyd, came running up to him. "Pa, a man just drove up to the house in a big automobile."

"Son," said the haggard farmer, "run back to the house as fast as your legs will carry you and ask that man what type of work he does. If he says he is a traveling minister, run down the cellar and lock up my liquor cabinet. If he says he is a law officer, lock the garage where I keep my still. If he says he is a salesman—sit on your ma's lap until I get there. . . ."

The saddest words of tongue or pen
Perhaps may be, "It might have been."
The sweetest words we know, by heck,
Are simply these: "Enclosed find check."

* * *

"How'd you do this week?"

"I got only three orders," said the salesman. "They were—'Get Out,' 'Stay out,' and 'Don't Come Back!' "

* * *

Did you hear about the salesman who was fired because his ulcer healed and his boss thought he'd lost interest in his work?

* * *

Dietrich, a young salesman, struck up a conversation with the man sitting next to him at the hotel bar. "I'm beginning to lose faith in my ability," he said. "Today was terrible! Not one sale. I've been thrown out of apartments, had doors slammed in my face, been kicked down stairs, had my samples thrown in the gutter, and been shot at by irate householders."

"What do you sell?" asked the man.

"Bibles," said Dietrich.

* * *

Stradford was returning home to Chicago from a trip through Illinois with eighteen hundred dollars, cash collected for orders, in his pocket. Just outside of Peoria he was stopped by a man in shabby, ill-fitting clothes. Stradford opened the door of his car and the guy got in. The hitchhiker soon revealed that he had just completed a six-year stretch for robbery.

The eighteen hundred dollars felt very insecure in Stradford's pocket. With a flash of inspiration he stamped on the accelerator and brought the car up to ninety miles an hour.

For once, a motorcycle cop stopped the car and gave Stradford a ticket to appear in court—the following Friday. In vain the salesman pleaded to be taken to jail right away. The cop left.

For the rest of the ride into Chicago Stradford was miserable. The eighteen hundred was as good as gone. Suddenly, the passenger said, "This is it, buddy." The salesman stopped the car. The robber stuck out his hand. There was no gun in it.

"Thanks for the lift," he said. "I guess this is the least I could do."

And he handed Stradford the cop's black leather summons book.

* * *

SELLING SONG

She was only a salesman's daughter
but she gave out plenty of samples.

* * *

Horowitz rang a Houston doorbell and it was answered by a beautiful blonde in a see-through silk robe.

"Pardon me," he said, "but I have a number of handy household items you might be interested in."

"Ah'd love to see them,"she answered, leaning over and revealing perfect breasts.

"Now you take these new-fangled potato peelers," he continued, while she allowed the robe to creep open a little showing a pink thigh. "They're very economical," he said.

Then she let the robe fall completely open displaying all of her charms. "Why don't yew step inside. Ah think ah hear someone coming," she whispered, allowing the robe to remain open.

Horowitz stepped inside. She closed the door.

"Which part of me do you think is the most sensitive?"

"Your ears."

"My ears?" she asked.

"Yes," he replied, " 'cause that was me you just heard coming!"

* * *

Denton, the door-to-door salesman, was making a pretty good buck until his competitor decided to put only schoolboys on the route. Then business fell off sharply.

Denton thought about the problem for a while and finally hit on a solution. The next time he rang a doorbell he said, "Good morning, madam. I'm working my son's way through college."

* * *

Some fellas were hanging around a lonely Arizona desert gas station when they spied a tiny dust cloud on the horizon. Swiftly a car approached and came to a screeching halt. Fenster, a traveling salesman, jumped out of the car and raced into the men's room. Instantly there came violent noises: whistling, tootings, rumblings, splashings, and thuddings.

One of the yokels said, "He sure musta had to go real bad."

Another country bumpkin approached the closed door of the john and said, "Hey mister, that was a pretty good movement."

Weakly from within came the salesman's voice. "If you think that was something, just wait'll I get my pants down."

* * *

An insect-repellent salesman wanted an order so badly he made farmer Corbus a special proposition. "I'll strip completely, spray myself with my company's product, and then spend the night lashed to a chair in the pasture. If I don't get bitten, you give me the order; if I do, I'll pay you fifty bucks!"

The farmer said, "Okay." Next morning when he untied the salesman he was amazed to see he had no bite marks. But the poor guy was in a state of near exhaustion.

"What happened?" asked Corbus.

The salesman said, "Well, the insects weren't any trouble, but tell me, doesn't that damn calf have a mother?"

Garfinkel sold strawberries from his truck in the suburbs of Philadelphia. He knocked on the door of a house and said, "You wanna buy some strawberries?"

"Come around back," said a ravishing redhead.

Garfinkel went to the rear, rang the bell, and the woman opened the door. Garfinkel froze in shock. She was stark naked. Not a stitch of clothing on. Garfinkel started to cry.

"What's the matter?" asked the redhead.

"Today my wife ran away with my best friend," he explained, "I lost $3,000 in the stock market, and now you're gonna screw me out of my strawberries."

* * *

Garner had his prospect backed up against a wall. "Take our accident insurance policy," he insisted.

"Why should I?" he asked.

"Listen!" boasted the salesman. "One month ago a man took out a policy with us. The other day he broke his neck and we paid him $10,000. Now think! Tomorrow *you* may be the lucky one!"

* * *

Did you hear about the insurance salesman who claims his greatest successes are with young housewives who aren't adequately covered?

* * *

Barbara traveled with a line of cosmetics, and one night in a storm she was forced to stop at a farmhouse. The farmer's two sons, Zeke and Lem, were youths. She decided to have both of them.

After supper she took them out in the barn and incited them to have intercourse with her. At the crucial moment she took out two rubbers.

"What are them things?" asked Zeke.

"If you wear these," said Barbara, "you won't be worried about pregnancy or venereal diseases."

Three days later Zeke asked his brother, "You pregnant?"

"No," replied Lem.

"Got any venereal disease?"

"No."

"Well, then, let's take these damn things off. I got to piss or I'll explode!"

* * *

Dexter and Jason, two Yuppie attorneys, were comparing notes on the women employees in their Beverly Hills law firm. "Does Louise the receptionist fool around?"

"I wouldn't want to say she's promiscuous," said Jason, "but Louise is the only girl I ever dated who has a condom-vending machine on the wall of her john."

* * *

Miss Zabinski was in the pleasure-selling business. On the way to Las Vegas her car broke down on a muddy country road, and a passing farmer stopped to fix it for her. Afterwards she offered to give him a little pleasure in return.

She laid down on the back seat, hiked up her skirt, and he started to climb on top. Then he remembered his lunch was in a pocket of his overalls. Not wanting to squash his victuals, he pulled the bag out, and the food spilled everywhere. But he caught what he could before it hit the floor.

The Polish girl saw what was in his hand and muttered, "I've been all over the world, and done it all kinds of ways, but this is the first time I've ever had a farmer try to sop it up with a biscuit!"

* * *

Finkelman refused to leave when the secretary told him the boss was out. An hour passed, then two. Finally, weary of being a prisoner in his own office, the boss admitted the salesman. "My secretary told you I was out," said the puzzled boss. "How'd you know I was in?"

"Easy," explained Finkelman. "Your secretary was working."

* * *

TYPIST
TITTERS

Typist Titters

Rosita, a cute nineteen-year-old Puerto Rican, was about to apply for a secretarial job. She asked her friend Cathy, a secretary for several years, for some advice. "What should I say," inquired Rosita, "if they ask what my job qualifications are?"

"The truth," Cathy counseled. "Tell them you can type fifteen words a minute—if the wind is with you."

* * *

Did you hear about the Puerto Rican secretary who is getting so experienced she can now type twenty mistakes a minute?

* * *

Boss:	Were there any phone calls for me while I was out to lunch?
New Secretary:	Only one, but it was a crank call.
Boss:	What do you mean?
New Secretary:	A lady called and said, "Long distance from Rome to New York? I said, "It sure is," and hung up!

* * *

Sackowitz called Kay, his pretty, young secretary, into his office, locked the door, and said, "As I already told you, you're the loveliest thing in this company."

Visions of a mink coat passed through Kay's mind.

"Furthermore," continued the boss, "you dress nicely, and all my friends think I'm lucky to have you at my beck and call."

"Oh, thanks," murmured Kay.

"Well, you can forget all that," said Sackowitz, "because right now we are going to discuss your spelling, punctuation, and typing."

* * *

PRIVATE SECRETARY

A good one never misses a period.

* * *

In exasperation the manager finally said, "Miss Kowalski, why don't you answer the telephone?"

"I just get fed up," said the Polish girl. "Nine times out of ten it's for you."

* * *

An advertising executive who was swamped with work called his secretary.

"Look, Miss Murphy," he said, "don't put through any calls to me this morning. I'll be incommunicado."

"All right," said the Irish girl, "but in case anything very important comes up, hadn't you better let me have your phone number there?"

* * *

Rita Kent, the former Canadian Diplomatic Corps exec sec, tells about the typist interviewing for a job:

"I hope that you thoroughly understand the importance of punctuation," asked the personnel director.

"Oh, yes," she replied, "I always come to work on time!"

* * *

Art Gliner, the witty Washington, D.C. DJ warms up audiences with this tail wagger:

Baldwin's relatives were all gathered to hear the reading of his will. In a far corner sat curvy Miss Kenyon, Baldwin's secretary for the last two years. The lawyer had almost finished, and so far there had been no mention of the truly desirable Miss Kenyon who was now perched on the edge of her chair listening intently.

"And finally," read the attorney, "to Miss Kenyon, my beautiful but uncooperative secertary, whom I promised to remember: 'Hello there, Miss Kenyon!"

Tilford's secretary Miss Gridowski just could not seem to make it in on time, so he suggested she see a doctor.

Armed with the pills the M.D. had prescribed, the Polish girl went home, got to bed early, slept well, and awoke at dawn feeling much refreshed.

Miss Grabowski walked into the office five minutes early, beamed at her boss, and said, "I had no trouble getting up this morning."

"That's good," he replied, "but where were you yesterday?"

* * *

Andrea turned to her friend from the typing pool. "I've taken all the insults from my boss I'm gonna take. . . ."

She thought for a moment and said, "How do you spell 'quit'?"

* * *

Did you hear about the inventive Italian steno who somehow wired her personal vibrator to her bedside FM set and came up with the world's first radio alarm cock?

* * *

Fishman said to his new secretary, ''Miss Dandridge, always add a column of figures at least three times before you show me the result.''

The next day she came in with a big smile. ''Mr. Fishman,'' said the girl, ''I added these figures ten times.''

''Good, I like a girl to be thorough.''

''And here,'' she said, ''are my ten answers.''

* * *

Jane, Alice, and Nelli were talking about how tired they'd been after working overtime the night before.

Jane groaned, ''I was so bushed when I got home, I fixed myself a bite, took my bath, and went straight to bed.''

''You call that weary?'' sneered Alice. ''I showered and sacked out without stopping to eat.''

''You guys don't know what tiredness is,'' said Nelli. ''I dragged up the stairs, unlocked my door, didn't chew, didn't screw, skipped the washup, too . . . just flopped on top of my cot. Next thing I knew it was almost 2:00, and there was an awful racket and scratching at my door. I got up, looked outside, and there was my butt just dragging itself home.''

* * *

What's the difference between a stenographer and a secretary?

A stenographer watches her commas, and a secretary watches her periods.

* * *

He: Would you say "yes" to being my secretary at $500 a week?
She: A dozen times a day if necessary!

* * *

Charlene and Donna were having lunch at MacArthur Park, the "in" San Francisco watering hole.

"Where did you get the beautiful fur coat?" asked Charlene.

"Bought it," replied Donna.

"How can you afford it?"

"Time payments. I give the shop owner a little each week."

* * *

There was a young typist named Valerie
Who started to count every calorie.
Said her boss in disgust,
"If you lose half your bust,"
Then you're worth only half of your salary."

* * *

The office vamp bragged, ''I went out with a millionaire from Texas last night, and what do you think he gave me? Five hundred dollars!''

''Wow,'' said the girl at the next desk. ''That's the first time I heard of a $498 tip!''

*   *   *

Phoebe, the knockout new steno gave a piece of paper to the company bookkeeper and said, ''Here's the report you wanted, Mr. Bickard.''

''My name is Mr. Pickard,'' he corrected. ''You must have been talking to the marketing director, who can't pronounce his P's right. What else did he say about me?''

''Well,'' she replied, ''only that when it comes to meaningless details, you're a regular *Brick*. . . .''

*   *   *

''Did you pick up any Italian on your vacation?'' Gloria asked Deborah at the next desk.

''I'll say I did,'' enthused Deborah.

''Let me hear you say some words.''

''I didn't learn any words.''

*   *   *

When Jennifer, the superbly stacked secretary, entered her boss's office one morning, he looked out the window and remarked, "It's certainly going to be a beautiful day."

"I don't think so," Jennifer replied. "The weather forecast is for snow."

"It's not going to snow," contradicted the exec. "I'll lay you twelve to one."

"I'd rather not," she retorted. "That's my lunch hour."

* * *

Pauline got married and then left the company to have a baby. A few months later she was having a drink with Rhoda, one of the girls still at the office. "Would you believe it," complained Rhoda, "I'm making the same salary as when I started two years ago!"

"Nursing a baby is a lot like getting a raise from your boss," advised Pauline. "It takes suction."

* * *

In the race toward matrimony, many a lucky secretary finds herself on the last lap.

* * *

Caroline was pregnant, and with her usual sense of humor left this note of resignation for her boss:

DEAR MR. RICHARDS,
I'M AFRAID I'M GETTING TOO BIG FOR THIS JOB.

* * *

There was a young steno named Mabel,
Who said, "I don't think that I'm able.
But I'm willing to try—
So where shall I lie;
On the bed, on the floor, or the table?"

* * *

Miss Kubick, a pretty secretary, just returned from a magnificent vacation in South America. She walked into the foreign-exchange section of her Detroit bank and dropped a wad of foreign currency on the counter. The teller counted it carefully and gave her 68 cents in exchange.

"Do you mean to tell me that's all I get?" gasped the Polish girl.

"I'm afraid so," said the teller. "That's the legal exchange rate."

"Damn. And like a fool I gave him breakfast, too."

* * *

Lisa Walter, the nifty northern California book rep, loves this nugget of nonsense:

Abigail had worked in the steno pool for years and jealously watched each of her co-workers march down the aisle. Now, as the last remaining bachelor girl, she showed up one Monday morning and began passing out cigars to all.

"What's the big idea?" asked the other girls.

Proudly she displayed a diamond ring and crowed, "It's a boy! Six feet tall and weighs 190 pounds."

Gladys and Tillie were chatting in the company cafeteria. "Oh, this night life is killing me!" sighed Gladys.

"Ain't it the truth," agreed Tillie. "I tell you, I hate the very thought of one man after another making love to me night after night. I'll be glad when I've had enough of it!"

* * *

SECRETARY

A girl you pay to learn to type while she is searching for a husband.

* * *

Did you hear about the free-loving secretary who says that two martinis usually make her feel like a new man?

* * *

"I'm so tired," complained the pretty career girl to her friend. "Last night I didn't sleep until after three."

"No wonder you're tired," her friend replied. "Twice is usually all I need."

* * *

Inez and Yolanda met at the apartment laundry room.

"I think my boss is getting interested in me," announced Inez.

"How can you tell?" asked Yolanda.

"Today he asked me to go and get measured for a diaphragm."

* * *

Cynthia and Doris, two former exec secs, were sipping rum punches at a Palm Beach country club.

"Why are you so down today?" asked Cynthia. "You look like you've lost your last friend."

"I'm so ashamed," said Doris. "And you mustn't breathe a word, but I caught my husband screwing around."

"Don't let it bother you," snapped Cynthia. "That's how I caught mine."

* * *

If skirts get any shorter,
Said the typist, with a blush,
There'll be two more cheeks to powder
And a lot more hair to brush!

* * *

Did you hear about the cute secretary who preferred tall men because the bigger they are, the harder they ball?

* * *

Eighty percent of secretaries are touch typists . . . what are the other twenty percent?

Hunt 'n peckers.

* *

OFFICE X'MAS PARTY

The best opportunity for a secretary to get a raise by lying down on the job.

* * *

B. J. Hardy, the terrific Gualala typist, tells about the Tulsa oil magnate who fell in love with his secretary, but was appalled by her ignorance of literature so he tried to improve her IQ. One morning she walked into his office and said, "I took your advice. I read a book last night!"

He said, "That's fine. What was the title?"

She said, "*Dun and Bradstreet!*"

* * *

Did you hear about the gorgeous absentminded secretary who left her clothes at the office and took her boss to the cleaners?

* * *

Finestein decided to put his secretary Susan in her place. After all, business was business.

"All right!" he said. "We went to bed together a few times, so what? Who told you you could come in late just because you're getting fat?"

"Two people told me," said Susan. "My doctor and my lawyer."

* * *

The secretary, big and buxom, phoned her mother to inform her, "I'll be late home for dinner tonight, Mom. I made a mistake last night and the boss wants me to do it over again."

* * *

"How are you on the typewriter?" the boss asked the new girl.

"Gosh, I don't know," replied the girl. "I've never tried it in that position."

* * *

After three years with a Houston oil company, Marion, a stunning steno, was transferred to the company's Dallas office. The morning she reported to her new desk, Caldwell, the president, invited her into his office and said, friendly-like, "I hope you'll be happy working with us. We'll expect about the same of you here as you've been accustomed to in Houston."

"Yes, suh," she replied, "that's what ah'd anticipated. Do yew mind if ah hang mah blouse over this chair?"

Efficient secretaries are scarce. A good one can make over two hundred dollars a week. There's no limit to what a bad one can make.

* * *

A buxom young typist named Baynes
At her work took particular pains.
She was good at dictation
And long explanations,
But she ran more to bosom than brains.

* * *

Roxanne, a centerfold-like blonde was explaining to her roommate why she spent two weeks in Acapulco with her boss.

"He's gonna give me 500,000 palarados!" she said.

"Palarados?" said her friend. "We don't have money like that!"

"I know," said Roxanne, "but if we ever do I'll be rich!"

* * *

Boss: Miss Zalinski, why is there a frankfurter behind your ear?

Miss Zalinski: Oh my gosh! I must've eaten my pencil for lunch!

* * *

Pretty Polly, the new stenographer, was being given no peace by Vito, a Neanderthal type from shipping. He fancied himself the company lover, and finally she couldn't take it any longer.

"Look," Polly said one day when Vito stopped at her desk, "have you heard the story about how to keep an asshole in suspense?"

"No, I haven't, baby," said the Italian.

"In that case," she snapped, "I might just tell it to you next week!"

* * *

A Chicago Yuppie ad exec interviewing applicants for the position of private secretary nearly fainted when Vanessa showed up. She combined some of the best physical and mental features of Bo Derek, Farrah Fawcett, and Madame Curie. But he told himself, "You must not expose yourself to temptation—and besides, your wife will murder you."

So he sighed and told the girl, "I'm afraid you won't do."

She looked at him and whispered, "Won't do what?"

* * *

Cora Sue, an Atlanta receptionist, picked up her desk phone and a man on the other end said, "I'd like to speak to Mr. Sexour."

"What was that?" she asked.

"I want to talk to Mr. Sexour."

"I'm sorry, I can't understand you."

"For heaven's sake," the man shouted. "Don't you have a Sexour there?"

"Sir," replied the girl, "we don't even have a coffee break."

* * *

"I was interviewed in depth this afternoon for a secretarial job," Irene told her roommate.

"You mean for more than an hour?"

"No. By more than seven inches."

* * *

Bernice was telling one of the girls at the office about her first visit to a nudist camp. "I showed up with nothing on but a few leaves," said Bernice.

"But I thought a nudist wore nothing!"

"That's just it," explained Bernice. "It was autumn when I went and the leaves were falling."

* * *

Question: ''How do you punctuate this sentence: 'fun fun fun worry worry worry'?''

Answer: ''Fun period, fun period, fun no period; worry, worry, worry?''

* * *

With office floors all mirror waxed
And polished to perfection,
The typist in her teeny skirt
Makes a striking new reflection.

* * *

''You know,'' said the gossip-loving office cutie to her lunch companion, ''I'd *never* say anything about Sherry unless I could say something good. And, sister, is this *good*. . . .''

* * *

Heather: Vickie told me that you told her the secret I told you not to tell her.

Phoebe: Gee, and I told her not to tell you that I told her.

Heather: Well, I told her I wouldn't tell you she told me, so don't tell her I told you.

* * *

Barbara, Gwen, and Rena were sitting at their desks typing reports. "I don't have to do this, you know," bragged Barbara. "I was a very wealthy lady. I had three mink coats, a jewelry box full of diamond rings, and a big Cadillac."

"Well, you don't really think I have to do this, do you!" snapped Gwen. "At one time, I lived in a house with two swimming pools, and I had a butler, a maid, and a closet full of furs."

Rena sat before her typewriter trying desperately to type with just two fingers. Finally, she said, "Look, ladies, I did a little hooking on the side myself but where the hell did you learn how to type?"

IDEAL STENOGRAPHER

One that sits on the boss's lap and bawls till his business goes in the hole.

* * *

Collins, the big boss, noticed a perky little stacked-up file clerk and invited her into his office. After some small talk he said, "If you'll make oral love to me, I'll see to it that you're promoted next month."

"What do you take me for?" reacted the girl. "I don't swallow that stuff!"

* * *

Did you hear about the smart steno who never asks the boss for advances on next week's salary?

She asks him for salary on next week's advances.

* * *

Amanda: Hasn't the shipping manager got a handsome profile?

Mildred: That's no profile. He's got a deep pants pocket. Those are his keys.

* * *

One day, after a phone call from his wife, the braggart office manager strutted into the steno pool, chest puffed out with self-satisfaction, and proclaimed loudly, "Well, girls, my wife is pregnant!"

From the back of the room a small voice replied, "Who do you suspect?"

* * *

Patricia, an exec sec with a large Chicago legal firm, was showing off her new mink coat. "How do I look?" she asked her best friend.

Responded her pal, "Guilty!"

* * *

Did you hear about the legal secretary who told her amorous boyfriend, "Stop and/or I'll slap your face?"

* * *

"How's that new Puerto Rican typist working out?"

"Well, she's very very slow. Mainly because every time the bell on her machine tinkles she knocks off for a cup of coffee."

* * *

The new secretary was telling her employer about her last job. "If you must know," she explained, "my last boss fired me because of the mistake I wouldn't make."

* * *

Bertha and Emily were on a break from the typing pool. "Why are you so upset?" asked Bertha.

"I was shocked to find Arnold with another woman," sobbed Emily. "It was his wife."

* * *

Amy, Linda, and Nicole applied for the job of secretary to the president, and the company psychologist put to them one main question: "How much is two and two?"

"Four," said Amy.

"Forty-four," said Linda.

"Four or maybe forty-four," said Nicole.

The shrink took the head of the company off to the side and said, "The first showed logic, the second imagination, the third showed both. Which do you choose?"

The president said, "I want the blonde with the big tits."

* * *

Boss: Miss Bolicki, will you please take a letter to Mr. Corwin in Los Angeles?

Secretary: Only if you promise to pay my bus fare.

* * *

When the struggling stenographer stops struggling, she often discovers that she doesn't have to be a stenographer.

* * *

STENO SONG

You're Like an Electric Typewriter and I Love the Way You Shift Your Carriage

FIRE
SALE

Business Banter

Schwartz and Weinstein were chatting in the steam room. "Is your son a good businessman?" asked Schwartz.

"My boy is so dedicated to his work," said Weinstein, "that he keeps his secretary near his bed in case he should get an idea during the night!"

* * *

Mandel and Seigel met at Ratner's for lunch. "How's business?" asked Mandel.

"Lousy!" answered Seigel. "On Monday, the whole day, I sold only one suit. Tuesday, business was so bad the salesmen were trying to sell each other. And Wednesday was even worse, yet."

"Why?"

"The man that bought the suit Monday brought it back!"

* * *

Posner rented space at one of those outdoor store fronts on the lower East Side of New York. A woman customer picked up a broken fork and asked, "How much?"

"A penny," said Posner.

"A penny!" grumbled the woman. "That's too much!"

"So make me an offer."

* * *

Skolnick owned a store in Detroit that had recently been burglarized. He met his friend Mintz on the street.

"I'm sorry to hear 'bout the robbery," said Mintz. "Did you lose much?"

"Some," replied the storekeeper. "But it would've been a lot worse if the burglar had broken in the night before."

"Why?" asked the friend.

"Well, you see," said Skolnick, "just the day of the robbery I marked everything down 20 percent."

* * *

SIGN IN WINDOW OF MIAMI
BANKRUPT DISCOUNT STORE

We Undersold Everybody

* * *

Zimmer the dress salesman covered the Midwest, and at his first stop in Chicago he checked into a hotel. In the middle of the night the place caught fire. Zimmer came running out on the street with nothing on—except an erection.

He stopped one of the firemen. "When you go inside," said Zimmer, "if you see a gorgeous blonde with big boobs and a nice behind, give her a screw—it's paid for already!"

* * *

Newman and Littner, two cloak-and-suit manufacturers, were sitting in their empty offices wailing over the sudden drop in business. "I wish Gabriel would blow his horn," said Newman.

"Why?" asked Littner.

"All the dead people'll come to life," explained Newman, "and they'll all need clothes."

* * *

Business is never really bad. In fact, it's a lot like sex. When it's good it's wonderful. And when it isn't so good, it isn't so bad either.

* * *

Plotkin went to a Las Vegas house of ill repute. He paid $100 and relieved himself. When he finished, Betty Lou his bedmate said, "That was great. You're the best I've had in a long time. If you want to go again, it's free."

Plotkin could not turn down such an offer. So he worked himself up, and once again released his pleasure.

When they finished, the girl said, "Mister, you're terrific! I enjoyed that so much that if you want to go again, I'll pay you $100."

Plotkin rested 15 minutes, but no matter how hard he played with himself, he couldn't get an erection. Finally he gave up. Plotkin grabbed his putz and said, "You son-of-a-bitch bastard. When it comes to spending a buck, you're all there; but when it comes to making a dollar . . . !"

* * *

Customer: What do you mean, $700 for that antique dresser! Last week you only wanted $450.

Lefkowitz: Well, you know how the cost of labor and materials keeps going up.

* * *

Did you hear about the retired brassiere manufacturer who still liked to keep his hand in the business?

* * *

Miss Turnbull stood before her department supervisor shaking with anger.

"I just found out that Armstrong makes more money than I do!" she cried.

"I'm afraid it's true," said the supervisor, "but you see—"

"But nothing! Do he and I have the same job?"

"Yes, but . . ."

"Am I his equal in every task, and better than him in most?"

"Yes, but . . ."

"Then why on earth does he make more money than me?"

"His mother owns the company."

* * *

A stockbroker who paid more attention to his business than his wife came home one day and found her in the arms of a stranger.

"What is the meaning of this?" he demanded.

"It wasn't in *The Wall Street Journal*, dear," she said, "but I've gone public."

* * *

Ralph Visell, the lovable longtime Macy's exec, gets big laughs with this lulu:

Blumenthal, a dress manufacturer from New York's garment district, had to make a business trip which took him through Syria.

At the Syrian customs check-in an official frowned at the American. "Are you a Jew?" he asked.

"Of course not!" exclaimed the New Yorker.

"Well, what is your religion?"

"I'm a Seventh Avenue Adventist!"

An American textile buyer told a long but amusing anecdote at a luncheon in Seoul, Korea. The translator repeated it to the group in just a few words, and the audience laughed and applauded.

Later, the textile buyer commented, "I think it was wonderful the way they appreciated my joke. It's amazing how you were able to shorten it in Korean."

"Not at all," replied the interpreter. "I merely said, 'American with big checkbook has told funny story. Do what you think is appropriate.' "

* * *

Why do bald dress manufacturers have holes in their pockets?

So they can run their fingers through their hair!

* * *

"I can't understand why you failed in business."

"Too much advertising."

"You never spent a cent in your life on advertising."

"That's true, but my competitor did."

* * *

Tax Inspector: What's this claim for a trip to Miami for medical reasons?

Dress Manufacturer: That's because my creditors wouldn't let me breathe here.

* * *

Castillo, the clerk at the cigar counter, was preoccupied with a book. Goodwin waited and waited for service, but Castillo failed to notice him.

"I'd like some cigars," said the potential customer.

The Puerto Rican still ignored him.

"Hey, you," shouted Goodwin, "I'd like some cigars!"

"Help yourself," muttered Castillo. "I'm busy."

Goodwin picked out three cigars and tossed some change on the counter.

"May I ask just one question?" he inquired as he was leaving.

"Um, sure," grunted Castillo, "go 'head."

"Just what is that book you seem so interested in?"

"This?" replied the Puerto Rican. "Oh, it's a course in salesmanship."

* * *

"I can't understand it," said Matson to his partner, Finley. "Here we are bankrupt, through, finished—and only yesterday the president said that business was booming!"

"Maybe," said Finley, "the president has a better location!"

* * *

Ferris was watering his front lawn when he saw Sandler scurrying by.

"Hey, where are you going?"

"I'm off to visit a house of ill repute," replied Sandler.

"I'm surprised at you," said Ferris. "You're going to a whorehouse?"

"No, an advertising agency."

* * *

Pearlman was selling his poker buddy a suit. "I'm telling you, Mel," he said, "that even your best friend won't recognize you in that suit! Just take a walk outside for a minute and get the feel of it."

Mel went out and returned a moment later. Pearlman rushed up to him.

"Good morning, stranger," he beamed. "What can I do for you?"

* * *

"Harry, I'm in big trouble. I'm gonna go bankrupt—unless I can raise some cash—and I haven't the slightest idea where I'm going to get it from."

"I'm glad to hear it," said his friend. "For a minute there I was afraid you might think you could borrow it from me!"

* * *

Miklos sold hot dogs from a cart on Fifth Avenue. "How's business?" asked an acquaintance.

"Could be worse!" said the Greek. "I put away already two thousand dollar in the bank!"

"That's good," said the friend. "Maybe you lend me five dollars?"

"I not allowed!"

"Why not?"

"I make agreement with bank. They agreed not to sell hot dogs if I promise I no make loans!"

* * *

Customer: Is this suit all wool?
Edelman: I won't lie to you. It's not. The buttons are made of leather.

* * *

Greg Chapman, the charming Beverly Hills Executive Clothes exec, gets big boffs with this beaut:

Stern and Vogel owned a clothing store. When Stern returned from vacation at the Concord Hotel, he was horrified to find his partner bandaged from head to toe, walking on crutches.

"What happened?" he asked.

"You remember the orange-and-pink striped suit with the black lapels we've been stuck with for years?" said Vogel. "I sold it!"

"So, what happened to you? The customer didn't like the suit?"

"The customer loved the suit," said Vogel, "but the seeing eye dog nearly killed me!"

Maloney went to Hockman's Haberdashery to buy a new suit for a wedding.

"You look like a real gentleman," said Hockman. "Why don't you let me custom make you a special suit to order?"

"I don't think so," said the customer.

"Just tell me what kind of material you like, and I'll write to England. They'll get the wool, then they'll weave the cloth, and ship it over. I make a pattern, you'll come in for two or three fittings, and the suit'll be gorgeous!"

"But I need the suit in three days."

"Don't worry! You'll have it!"

* * *

The movie industry, like most businesses, has its share of nepotism. At one time, the head of a large studio brought in the boy who had married his daughter, and made him production chief.

Within nine months, the young man produced three films that were financial disasters. The father-in-law called him into his office. "It's not bad enough," he screamed, "the movies you made were lousy. And that you lost millions of dollars. But you set the son-in-law business back twenty years!"

* * *

McDowell, a truck driver from Philadelphia making his first trip to New York, saw the sign:

CLIMB ONE FLIGHT AND
SAVE $50 ON A NEW SUIT.

The Irishman climbed and was immediately shown a number of shoddy garments by Garfinkel the eager salesman. McDowell refused to bite.

Garfinkel knew that Edelman, the boss, was watching him, so he made a special effort with the next number. Garfinkel whirled the customer around and around before the mirror, crying, "It fits like a glove! You look like a movie star!"

When the Irishman again said, "No," Edelman took over, produced one blue serge suit, and made the sale in five minutes. As McDowell left, the boss said, "You see how easy it is when you know how? He went for the first suit I showed him."

"Yeah," agreed Garfinkel, "but who made him dizzy?"

* * *

"You bastard!" shouted Lou, "You've been sleeping with my wife!"

"Honest, Lou!" said his partner. "Not a wink!"

* * *

Balducci lived by the side of the road and sold hot dogs. He had trouble with his eyes so he didn't read the newspapers. He was hard of hearing so he had no television. But he sold good hot dogs.

He put up a sign telling how good they were. He stood by the side of the road and shouted, "Buy a hot dog, Mister?" And people bought. He increased his meat and bun orders. He bought a bigger stove to take care of his trade. He even brought his son home from college to help him.

But then something happened. His son said, "Pop, haven't you been listening to television? There's a big recession on. The European situation is terrible. The domestic situation is even worse."

Well, Balducci thought, "My son has-a been to college. He should know what's going on."

So the Italian cut down on his meat and bun orders. He stopped all his advertising. And he no longer bothered to stand on the road and sell his frankfurters.

His hot-dog sales fell almost overnight. One day he turned to his boy and said, "Son, you right, we certainly in the middle of a big-a recession!"

* * *

Rifkin closed his shop Friday night and headed for Jewish services, not realizing his fly was unzipped. At the temple entrance, he met Mrs. Markowitz, the president of the Ladies' Auxiliary. "I don't like to say nothin'," she said shyly, "but your business is open!"

"You're mistaken, lady!" said Rifkin.

"Believe me," said Mrs. Markowitz blushing, "your business is open!"

"You're crazy!" shouted Rifkin, rushing inside. "I close the store every Friday to come here!"

Later, at home, Rifkin saw that his fly was open and realized that Mrs. Markowitz had only been trying to tell him so in a delicate way. He telephoned her immediately.

"I wanna apologize!" he said, also trying to be tactful. "But tell me somethin'. When my business was open, was my salesman in or out?"

* * *

Feiler retired to Orlando where, one winter, he was pleased to run into an old friend from New York. "How was business this past season?"

"Business was so bad the dress manufacturers were firing their sons-in-law."

* * *

Eckstein and Adler, two clothing manufacturers, were sitting in a restaurant during the slack season.

"Did you hear about Milton?" asked Eckstein. "His place burned down."

"Yeah?" said Adler. "He's a nice fellow. He deserves it."

* * *

One morning Miss Wilson turned to her class and asked, "All those pupils who want to go to heaven, raise your hands."

All hands except little Barry's went up.

The teacher asked him, "Don't you want to go to heaven?"

"I heard my father tell my mother 'Business has gone to hell,' " replied Barry, "and I want to go where the business went."

* * *

"What do you think of all the women coming into the business world?"

"Look, no matter how many positions formerly held by men are taken over by women, there'll always be one opening that only a man can fill."

* * *

Dinkleman and Mrs. Krantz owned sheet factories next door to each other. Their products were about equal, and their prices about the same, but for some reason Mrs. Krantz had never been able to sell anything to a large department-store chain, while Dinkleman sold heavily to them. Finally, one day at a Chamber of Commerce luncheon, she cornered him and asked why.

"That buyer's a strange guy," said Dinkleman. "He comes into the shop and won't even talk to anybody but me. He'll sit around the waiting room for hours on end until I get to him, and never say a word."

"That must be a real snap sale," said Mrs. Krantz.

"No, once he sees me, it's all business again," replied her competitor. "He won't buy a thing until he's tested it. Says he has to be sure it can be slept on. So we go into my inner office, make up the sofa bed with our latest line, then we both put on pajamas and crawl in."

The lady laughed, "Tell me, does he snore?"

"Worse than that," said Dinkleman. "He takes my head and pushes it to the middle of the bed."

"What do you do then?" she asked.

"What can I do? He's my best customer."

* * *

In the old West when train robbing was at its height, Silverstein, a ribbon salesman from New York, became a luckless victim.

As the robbers went through the pockets of the passengers, Silverstein pulled out $200, but quickly took $4 from the pile and placed it in his vest pocket.

"What'd you do that for?" asked the holdup man, waving his revolver.

"My friend," replied the salesman, "certainly you wouldn't refuse me 2 percent discount on a strictly cash transaction like this?"

"Nate, you took your son-in-law into the dress business with you, how's he doin'?"

"It's amazing," said Jake. "He's been with me now only two weeks and already he's a month behind in his work!"

* * *

Furriers, Spiro, and Pincus met in Miami. "You took your son, the college boy, into the business. How's he working out?"

"You wouldn't believe it!" replied Pincus. "He's got an idea, he wants to cross mink with kangaroos to get fur coats with pockets in them!"

* * *

Nathan and Ira had been partners for years and now Ira lay dying. Nathan stood at his hospital bedside. "I have a confession to make," said Ira. "I robbed our firm of $100,000. I sold the secret formula to our competitors. I took the letter from your desk that your wife needed to get her divorce. And Nathan, I . . ."

"It's all right," said his partner. "It was me that poisoned you!"

* * *

SIGN IN KLUGMAN'S CLOTHING STORE WINDOW

Use Our Easy Credit Plan:
100 Percent Down
Nothing to Pay Each Month

* * *

During the 30's in Germany a politician pleaded with Hitler not to mistreat the Jews. "You must accept the fact that they are very smart business people."

"Oh!" ranted Der Führer, "what makes you think they're so smart?"

"Come and I'll show you."

He took the Nazi dictator to Holtzman's Hardware Store and whispered, "Ask him for a *left*-handed tea pot."

Hitler did. Holtzman went to the back of his store, picked up a teapot—*turned it around*—and returned.

"You're in luck," said the Jewish shopkeeper, "I just happen to have one left."

When they were back on the street the politician said, "You see! That's what I mean about the Jews being so smart."

"What is so smart about that?" shouted Hitler. "He just happened to have one left!"

* * *

Brandon and Farrow, two motion-picture execs were lunching at Scandia.

"You and I use the same call girl and I happen to know she charges you, a bookkeeper, twice as much as me," said Brandon. "Don't you object?"

"Why should I?" said Farrow. "I use the double-entry system."

* * *

And in Dallas two oil-company execs were chatting in the steam room of their Health Club.

"Did yew hear what ole Fallon did with his secretary?"

"No!"

"Well, he'd been trying to make out with her for months but she kept turning him down!"

"So?"

"So, he stapled her tits together!"

"What?"

"Yeah, ole Fallon says his motto is: 'If you can't lick 'em—join 'em!' "

* * *

Corporate Cackles

Wearing her tightest cotton dress, sexy Angela applied for the receptionist's position at the chemical company's personnel department. She sat in the office of Bower, the man in charge.

"What would be the chances for advancement, Mr. Bower?" Angela inquired, pursing her thick, red lips.

"In my company, young lady," responded Bower, "a girl with your qualities could go up, up, up! Provided, of course," he added, "that she was willing to go down, down, down."

* * *

Early one morning Phyllis, the personal secretary of a handsome president, burst into his office in a rage. "Mr. Cleery, I've worked faithfully for you for three years," she said, "and I still don't have a name plate on my office door. Why not?"

Slowly rising from behind his desk, her boss unzipped his trousers and pulled out his manhood. "Phyllis," he replied, "I call this 'quality,' and in this organization the quality goes in before the name goes on."

* * *

Did you hear about the executive who fired his secretary because of lack of experience?

All she knew was typing, shorthand, and filing.

* * *

The young executive greeted his attractive secretary warmly as he entered the office. "Good morning, Norma," he said, tossing his briefcase on his desk. "I had a dream about you last night."

"Oh, did you?"

"No," her boss replied, "I woke up too soon."

* * *

Fletcher started work as a stockroom boy. Within six months he was promoted to salesman. In another six months he was upped to sales manager, and shortly thereafter he was made general manager.

A few days later Fletcher was called in by the president of the firm who explained he would retire soon and turn the presidency over to the newcomer.

"Thanks," said Fletcher.

"Thanks?" said the president. "You've been with the company less than two years. Is that all you can think of to say?"

"Well," said the boy, "thanks a lot, Dad."

* * *

First Banker: You're looking for a cashier? I thought you just hired a new cashier last week.

Second Banker: We did. That's the one we're looking for.

* * *

Did you hear about the young executive who spent three months finding a suitable secretary?

He knows it pays to have a good head on your shoulder.

* * *

''What's happening with that new secretary you hired last week?''

''I took her out to lunch the other day, and I discovered she was not the old-fashioned type. After two old-fashioneds she couldn't type.''

* * *

Sherrard, a factory owner decided to add more ethnic personnel to his staff by hiring a German, an Irishman, and a Chinese. He said to the German, ''Schmidt, I'm putting you in charge of production. I want you to make things more efficient around here.''

To the Irishman he said, ''Clancy, you'll be in charge of personnel. You can handle hiring and firing, and general morale problems.''

To the Chinese he said, ''Wong, I know you don't yet have command of the language, but in your job you won't need that. I am going to put you in charge of supplies.''

Three weeks later, Sherrard returned and asked, ''How is it going, Schmidt?''

''Vunderful, effrysink is goink shmoozly. Production is up sree-fold!''

''How are things going with personnel, Clancy?''

''Oh, everything is getting along just foine. People are all liking each other.''

"How's Wong doing with supplies?"

"I don't know," said Schmidt, "I haf not seen ze shentleman for sree veeks."

"Clancy, how's Wong doing in supplies?"

"I have no idea," replied the Irishman. "I haven't seen the little fella at all."

Sherrard began to worry. No one had seen Wong for three weeks. The owner looked all through the factory but couldn't find him. Then as he was walking through the warehouse, between large stacks of big boxes, suddenly the Chinese leaped down on him and shouted, "SUPPLIES!"

* * *

Marlene, a beautiful brunette, was thrilled to get a job as private secretary to an Atlanta corporation vice-president for $300 per week. Arriving at nine o'clock the next morning, she was immediately summoned to his office, where she learned that her responsibilities included making love to him.

"I guess I knew this would be part of the job," she sighed when they had finished. "But for $300 a week, I really can't object too much."

"Well, here's $3.75 for the past half hour," said the executive. "You're fired."

* * *

Randall, vice chairman of a communications board was also president of his college alumni association. When the football coach asked him to give some work to one of his ball players, Randall agreed wholeheartedly.

Kolinski showed up the next day. "Here's some paint and a brush, go out back and paint my porch," said the corporate head. "I'll give you $50 when you're finished."

Three hours later the Polish boy returned and said, "All finished."

"Great," said Randall, "have any problems?"

"No, sir," said the Polack, "but, you know, that wasn't a Porsche, it was a Mercedes Benz."

* * *

OVERHEARD AT A CORPORATE COCKTAIL PARTY

Blake: What is the ultimate test of courage?
Grant: Tell me.
Blake: Two cannibals having oral sex.

* * *

Six days shalt thou labour and on the seventh thou shalt labour longer for thou shalt be paid double time.

Chapter 5 *Verse* 7
Union Bible

EMPLOYEE PRAYER

The Union is my shepherd; I shall not work,

It makes me to lie down on the job; it leadeth me beside the still factories.

It restoreth my fringe benefits.

It leadeth me in the paths of disruption for its own sake.

Yea, though I walk through the valley of the shadow of dismissal,

I will fear no victimization: for the union is with me.

Its "restrictive practices" and "go-slows" they comfort me.

It prepareth a strike committee before me in the presence of my employers.

It anointeth my head with pay raises; my bank balance runneth over.

Surely shop stewards and union dues shall follow me all the days of my membership; and I shall dwell in a council house forever.

Morgan invited his pretty secretary out to dinner after they worked overtime. They went dancing, and then to her apartment to bed.

Much later, as he was leaving, he asked for a piece of chalk, which he put behind his ear and went home.

When his wife asked what had kept him so long, Morgan told her the truth. "We worked late so I took my secretary out to dinner, then we went back to her place and made love!"

"Liar!" she shrieked, "I know you were playing pool. You've still got the chalk behind your ear!"

Boss: Your salary is a personal matter not to be divulged to anyone.

New Executive: I won't say a word: I'm just as ashamed of it as you are.

* * *

Did you hear about the fast-rising executive who, on entering his newly decorated office, had his secretary on the carpet because she forgot to order a couch?

* * *

A plant turning out canned beans wanted to expand and Kieley, the market V.P., applied for advertising rates from one of the better magazines. He was told it would be fifty thousand dollars an issue. Kieley complained about the high price, to ballyhoo the beans.

"That's a bargain," stated the advertising man. "The Kotex people pay us eighty thousand for the same space per issue."

"That's all right for them," was the reply, "they're out for blood. We just want to fart around a little!"

* * *

Wife: Did you ask about promotion?

Husband: No, I forgot, probably due to all the excitement when I got the sack.

* * *

"Did you hear about DiAngelo?"
"No."
"He finally got a gorgeous secretary. She failed the typing test—but passed the physical."

* * *

In the corporate business world a Yes Man is a junior executive who always carries a tube of Vaseline in his briefcase in case the chairman of the board feels like staying after work.

* * *

A slick movie producer took his sexy secretary to his penthouse condo in Century City, ostensibly for the purpose of dictation. He showed her around and when they came to the bedroom, he quipped, "This is National Sex Week—would you care to contribute?"

She smiled and replied, "I already gave at the office."

* * *

GOOD EXECUTIVE

One who never puts off till tomorrow what he can get someone else to do today.

* * *

Phil Sevier, the personable Treasure Tours prexy, gets titanic titters from his travel clients with this tail wagger:

Tarzan came home in the afternoon and asked Jane for a triple Jack Daniels. He sat down and in a few moments finished off the drink. "Let me have another," ordered the ape man.

After a moment of hesitation, Jane blurted out, "Tarzan, I'm worried about your drinking. Every afternoon you come home and proceed to get totally sloshed."

"Jane, I can't help myself," Tarzan protested. "It's a jungle out there."

APOLOGY FROM A MAN FIRED FOLLOWING AN OFFICE PARTY

Dear Friends:

When I came into the office this morning, there was a general feeling of unfriendliness and, since several of you called me a dirty son-of-a-bitch to my face, I know I must have done something wrong at our office party last Friday. The office manager called me from the hospital this morning and made this my last day, so I would like to take this way of apologizing to all of you. I'd prefer speaking to everyone personally, but all of you seem to go deaf and dumb whenever I try to talk to you.

First, to our dear boss, Mr. Kimball, I'm sorry for all the things I called you Friday afternoon. I know your father is not a baboon, or your mother a Chinese whore. Your wife is a delightful woman and my story of buying her for fifty cents in Tijuana was strictly a figment of my imagination. Your children are undoubtedly yours, too. About the water cooler incident, I feel badly about it and I hope they didn't hurt your head when they were trying to get the glass jug off.

To Miss Grabowski, I express my deepest regrets. In my own defense I must remind you that you seemed to enjoy our little escapade on the stairway until the bannister broke and we fell eight feet to the second-floor landing. In spite of the rupture you incurred when I landed on top of you, I'm sure you will admit that when we landed, it was one of the biggest thrills you have ever had.

Mr. Wimmer, you old cuss, you've just got to forgive me for that little prank I played on you. If I had known you were goosey, I'd never have done it. It could have been a lot worse if that fat lady had not been standing right under the window you jumped through; she broke your fall a lot. People have been killed falling three stories.

Mr. McLain, I'm sorry I told the firemen it was you who turned in the false alarm. I had no way of knowing they would be such bad sports about it. Those fire hoses sure have a lot of pressure, don't they?

Andy Nelson, I know how you must have felt about me. Opening the door to the mop closet suddenly must have startled you and Miss Tooley quite badly. And when I think of how hard you bumped your chin on the sink when you bent over to pull up your pants, it makes me sick. We'll have to get together for dinner some night after the dentist finishes your plate.

Miss Quintero, the only excuse I can offer for stealing your clothes and hiding them when I found you had passed out in the Ladies' Room, is that I was drunk. Also, I want you to know that I was very embarrassed when I could not remember where I hid them, and you had to go home in that sofa cover. Running your panty hose up on the flag pole was a bit too much. . . . I was a little drunk.

To all the rest of you, I am sorry. Setting Mrs. Feinberg's lace panties on fire seemed a funny idea at the time. It makes me sad to hear that her husband is divorcing her because of it.

Peeing in everyone's drink was in bad taste, too, and not telling you until you all drank it was even worse.

Now that I've apologized and I know I'm forgiven, I have a big surprise for you. Even though I don't work here anymore, I'm going to do my damndest to get back to the office picnic next Friday.

Cordially,
Biff Barrington

* * *

During last winter's flu epidemic, a large firm sent its executives the following memo:

"Because of our shortened staff, will you please release your secretary for other's use when you are not taking advantage of her in your office?"

* * *

My typist's away on vAcattion
My typizt's away bg the seaz-
She lefft Me to do aiz the ty
pigg
O bRing bacck my typist to
me.
Md typiztm Is aw-py on vasc-
tion3
a fact gou can eaxily zee—
IT's odd how thees letirs get
mizxed up
Obrine back my tyspit to me;?
O Daxm!———P

* * *

First bloated capitalist: I've solved my lateness problem by giving all my workers a car.

Second bloated capitalist: How does that make any difference?

First bloated capitalist: They have to get there early to find a parking space.

* * *

The president of a baby-bottle company stood up before his staff and said, "We have 50,000 of these feeding bottles in stock, and we expect you salesmen to go out and create a demand."

Did you hear about the executive who is so old that when he chases his secretary around the desk, he can't remember why?

What is a corporate optimist?

A man who marries his secretary under the impression he can go on dictating to her.

* * *

"Okay, you're hired," said the busy executive, moving around his desk toward the buxom young female. "Now would you like to try for a raise?"

* * *

Ernie was the playboy of the company. He kept the typists bug-eyed with juicy tales of his conquests. One afternoon, Barlow, a bachelor in the office, asked, "Ernie, how do you do it? You're married. What's your secret?"

"It's simple," replied Ernie. "Tonight, take the 5:15 from Penn Station and get off at Great Neck. You'll find a dozen dolls waiting for their husbands. There are always some guys who work late. All you have to do is wait and let nature take its course."

That night Barlow boarded the 5:15 with Ernie's instructions fixed firmly in his mind. But he dozed off and didn't waken till two stops after Great Neck. He got off the train in a hurry and was about to catch a cab back to his destination, when he noticed a woman standing on the platform.

He approached her. They chatted, and soon Barlow asked whether she'd like to have a drink with him.

"I'd love to," she said, "but let's go to my place."

"They had some drinks, some dinner and then retired to the bedroom. They were going at it hot and heavy when the door swung open and the woman's husband entered.

"Jeezus, Margot!" he shouted, "what the hell is going on? So this is what you do when my back is turned! And as for you, you schmuck! I told you to get off at Great Neck!"

* * *

A well-stacked young advertising secretary wore tight knit dresses that showed off her figure, especially when she walked. Her young, aggressive boss motioned her into his office one afternoon and closed the door. Pointing to her tightly covered derriere, he asked, "Is that for sale?"

"Of course not!" she snapped angrily."

"Okay, then," he replied, "I suggest you quit advertising it."

* * *

Wedded Whimsy

Dirk and Quimby, two Yuppie ad biggies, were discussing the latest kitchen gadgets over a glass of Dom Perignon.

"Have you seen the machine that makes those ice cubes with a hole in them?"

"Hell, I married one!"

* * *

Jager and Marten, Houston investment counselors, were sipping Black Russians at the Shamrock Hotel lounge and battling over the charms of Bo Derek.

"I say she's overrated," said Jager. "Take away her eyes, her hair, her lips, and her figure and what have you got?"

"My wife," sighed Marten.

* * *

OVERHEARD IN COMPANY CAFETERIA

Arthur: What's up, Jeff? You look hassled.
Jeff: Yeah. I'm going to be a father.
Arthur: Congratulations! But what's so terrible about that?
Jeff: Nothing, except my wife doesn't know it yet.

* * *

Prescott, the utility company prexy, was telling about his recent experience. His wife was out of town, when their beautiful Colombian housemaid who sleepwalks came into his bedroom naked in the night.

"What did you do?"

"What could I do? I love my wife. I turned her around and headed her back to her own bed. What would you have done?"

"Exactly what you did, you lying son-of-a-bitch!"

* * *

RELATIVE HUMIDITY

The sweat that forms on your balls when you're caught screwing your sister-in-law.

* * *

Lockhurst and DeGraw, California computer eggheads, were having lunch. Said Lockhurst, "I'm thinking of asking Kay to marry me."

"Before you do, why not call marriage anonymous?" said DeGraw.

"What's that?"

"It's a great organization. You call them if you feel like proposing, and at 6:00 in the morning they send over two screaming five-year-olds and a woman in a ratty housecoat with curlers in her hair."

* * *

Richard, the board chairman of a department-store chain, sat beside the bed of his sick wife. They had been married for 18 years, and now that his wife had contracted a serious illness it seemed that the end was near.

The ailing woman looked up at her husband with tear-filled eyes and said, "Darling, I want you to promise me one thing. If I should die and you should ever remarry, please do not let your second wife wear any of my clothes."

"I promise," answered Richard. "Your clothes wouldn't fit Barbara anyhow."

* * *

Pennock, a Manhattan bank veep, was about to cross Fifth Avenue when he noticed a funeral procession coming down the street. Two hearses were traveling side by side. Behind them walked a man dressed in black with a huge Doberman pinscher straining on a leash. Behind him walked thirty men in single file.

In awe of the procession, Pennock sidled up beside the man with the dog and asked, "Whose funeral is this?"

"My wife's and mother-in-law's," he replied.

"What happened?"

"This dog killed them."

"Can I borrow it for a week?" asked the bank exec.

"Get to the end of the line!"

Mortal Funeral Home
Mortal Funeral

"You don't speak nicely to me the way you used to," Mrs. Kendrick said. "I guess you just don't love me anymore."

"Don't love you," muttered her husband. "There you go again, don't love you! Why, I love you more than life itself. Now shut up and let me read my book."

* * *

What's slower than your wife getting dressed?

A woman who isn't your wife getting undressed.

* * *

Did you hear about the Yuppie who married the corporate president's daughter and hung her nude picture over his desk?

He didn't want people to think he had married her just for her money.

* * *

"What's it like to be married to the boss's daughter?"

"The morning after our wedding she made some greasy eggs, burnt toast, half-raw bacon, and gummy coffee. . . . It was then I realized she couldn't cook either."

* * *

Ansen, the owner of a large factory in a small Ohio town, was being questioned by a woman reporter concerning his policy for hiring only married men to work for him.

"I think it's a good policy," she offered. "But as a wife, I can't help wondering why you hire married men only. Is it because we women have given them strength, understanding, and ambition?"

"No, it's because they're used to being pushed around, can obey orders instantly, and don't sulk when I yell at them!"

* * *

Caldwell, a middle-aged executive, became quite irritated by the constant ribbing he received from junior employees who kept making fun of his baldness. One morning, a new trainee had the gall to run his hand across Caldwell's pate while loudly exclaiming, "Feels just like my wife's ass!"

"You're right," he said, feeling his pate. "So it does, so it does."

* * *

Down on Wall St. they're all talking about the marriage of the dipsomaniac stockbroker and the nymphomaniac receptionist.

It was nip and fuck all the way.

* * *

"Sometimes my wife shows a sadistic streak."

"How so?"

"When I got home from my vasectomy operation the first thing she served me was oysters."

* * *

As Dobbins stepped off the scale, he said to his spouse, "Listen to this fortune: 'You are brilliant, resourceful, and energetic. Everything you touch will turn to gold.'"

The wife replied, "It got your weight wrong, too."

* * *

Perkins and Baxter were in the airport for their plane to the company's annual stock meeting in Atlanta.

"I was reading in *The Wall Street Journal* today," said Perkins over his fifth J&B, "about a lie detector they used on an executive applying for a job. It proved he was lying. Must be a wonderful thing. Did you ever see a lie detector?"

"See one?" said Baxter, "I married one!"

* * *

Wesley married the oil company president's daughter and decided to be a considerate bridegroom: he wasn't going to molest the bride the first night. Wesley lay on his side of the bed and, after a couple of hours, the bride looked over. Wesley had his eyes wide open. "Aren't you asleep, honey?" she asked.

"No," he replied.

"Is anything wrong?" she continued.

"I can't get to sleep," answered Wesley, "I've got such a hard-on that it's got my skin stretched so tight I can't close my eyes!"

* * *

The steel company president came home from work one evening and found his wife nude in front of a mirror, fondling and admiring her breasts.

"What's the idea?" he asked.

"Oh," she replied, "the doctor examined me today and told me that, for a woman of my age, I had the prettiest breasts he'd ever seen."

"Oh, yeah?" said the husband. "Well, what did he say about your big, fat ass?"

"Why darling," she said, "your name wasn't even mentioned."

* * *

A market researcher who was conducting a sex survey for a new birth-control product telephoned Eckert, one of the participating husbands.

"Sir, there's a discrepancy in your answers," said the researcher. "Under *Frequency of Intercourse,* you put *twice a week,* while your wife wrote *several times nightly.*"

"That's right," said Eckert, "but that's only until we get the second mortgage on our house paid off."

* * *

Milicent had been nagging her stockbroker husband for a mink coat for weeks. Finally she demanded, "Just when are you going to buy me a fur coat?"

"When you get hair on your chest," he replied.

With that, she pulled her skirt up to her waist and cried, "What do you call that?"

"You don't call that hair on your chest, do you?" he asked.

"Well," she answered, "before we were married, it was your hope chest. Since we've been married, it's been your tool chest. And now if I don't get a mink coat it's going to be a community chest!"

* * *

Louise had been trying to get her Yuppie husband to pay more attention to her. One night he came home from work and she greeted him with, "Notice anything different about me?"

"Yves St. Laurent dress?"

"No."

"Charles Jourdan shoes?"

"No. Something else."

"I give up."

"I'm wearing a gas mask."

* * *

"Why did you wait two weeks when your wife was sick before calling the doctor?"

"Well, she had laryngitis."

* * *

"My wife Fay and I have been married 18 years," boasted Feldman, "and she has been as faithful as the family pet."

"What are you talking about?" snorted Bortnick. "She's run away from you a hundred times."

"Yes, that's true . . . but she ALWAYS comes back!"

* * *

Mrs. Liddle reported her shipping-magnate husband missing, and then she became a daily visitor at the morgue. One day as the morgue attendant uncovered the face of a corpse, the woman thought she recognized her spouse, but she wasn't positive.

"Pull the sheet down a bit lower," she asked.

The attendant brought the sheet down to the waist, and asked, "Lady, is this your man?"

"I'm still not sure. Pull the sheet lower."

The attendant slipped and he pulled the sheet off entirely.

"Now, lady, is this guy your husband?"

"No." she replied, "No, he isn't—but somebody certainly lost a good friend!"

CITY
MORGUE

Plump Mrs. Harris at a Weight Watchers session confided to the woman sitting next to her.

"My husband insists I come here because he'd rather screw a trim-figured woman."

"Well, what's wrong with that?" asked her seatmate.

"It's just that he does it while I'm at these damn meetings!"

* * *

A real womanizing exec died. The undertaker phoned his wife to tell her that the corpse had an erection, and asked what he should do about it.

"Cut it off and shove it up his ass," she said. "That's the only place in town it hasn't been!"

* * *

Dixon and Grady, two Princeton fraternity brothers, were having a reunion.

"Gee," said Dixon, "you look sort of down, pal."

"I had everything a man could want," moaned Grady. "Money, a big house, the love of a beautiful and wealthy woman. Then, bang, one morning my wife walked in!"

* * *

Keller left the office and, upon arriving home, discovered his shapely wife in bed with a neighbor. "Since you're sleeping with my wife," shouted Keller, "I'm going over and sleep with yours."

"Go ahead," replied the neighbor. "You probably need the rest."

* * *

Dear Friend:

This chain was started in the hope of bringing happiness to all tired business men. Unlike most chains, it doesn't require money. Simply send a copy of this to five male friends, then bundle up your wife, and send her to the fellow whose name heads the list. When your name's reached the top of the list, you will receive 12,243 women and some should be corkers. Have faith. Don't break the chain. One man broke it and got his wife back.

Your friend,
Homebreakers, Ltd.

* * *

Nancy sued her husband for bigamy. "I'll teach the rat," she promised, "that he can't have his Kate and Edith, too!"

* * *

Did you hear about the Long Island wife of a corporate officer who says she suffers from marital thrombosis?

She is married to a clot.

* * *

Martha was peeved at the lack of attention on the part of her computer-software-company V.P. husband. She was trying to bait him as he sat engrossed in his newspaper.

"I was out with a man the other day," she stated.

No response.

"He thought I was awfully pretty," she continued, "and had a beautiful shape."

No response.

"I let him take off all my clothes and make love to me."

Still no response.

"He said it was the best he'd ever had."

Silence.

"He said the next time we had a party he was going to fill it with ice cream and eat it."

The paper dropped.

"Hell," shouted the man, "there isn't a man alive that could eat that much ice cream!"

* * *

Mrs. CEO: *(at 2 a.m.):* A fine time to come home. I want an explanation and I want the truth.

CEO: Make up your mind. You can't have both.

* * *

Marilyn had to do some shopping and didn't want to take Wesley, her small son, along, so she told him, "Now you stay and take care of Daddy for me, and be sure he behaves."

When she got home, she asked, "Was Daddy a good boy?"

"Daddy was fine, but the neighbor's cat got drunk," said Wesley.

She asked him what he meant, and he said, "Well, the lady next door brought her cat over to see Daddy in his den, and I heard him say, 'You've got the tightest pussy I've ever seen'!"

* * *

ATTENTION CORPORATE WIVES

If you try too hard to wear the pants around your house, you are liable to find your husband has located a girlfriend who doesn't wear any.

* * *

Marjorie decided to surprise her husband at his Wall Street office one afternoon. She walked unannounced into his inner sanctum and found him naked on the couch with his shapely, young secretary. "Don't try to explain," she hissed. "Let me guess! This is one of your *hard* days at the office, right?"

A phone company consumer-division head convinced his wife that they should move to a Connecticut farm. He would commute to work every day, and she could raise chickens.

One night two years later the woman announced, "I want to get four black roosters."

"What for?" asked the exec.

"I want to use them for pallbearers for the dead cock you bring home every night."

* * *

On a crowded crosstown bus, little David asked his mother in a loud voice, "Why did that lady put her titty in the baby's mouth?"

The conversation on the bus stopped in dead silence. The mother replied, "She's feeding him some milk."

"Did I ever get milk from you that way?" asked David.

She answered, blushing, "No dear, I fed you with a bottle."

"Does Daddy get milk like that?"

She whispered tensely, "No dear, I don't have any milk in me."

The little boy who had spent the morning at his father's law office, announced, "Daddy's secretary does. . . ."

* * *

A middle-aged book publishing exec and his wife checked into a Minneapolis hotel. After they turned out the light in their room, they looked across the hotel courtyard and saw two young newlyweds playing a game. The wife tried to throw a doughnut over her husband's penis, while he tried to throw a pickle into her vagina.

"Let's try it," said the publisher.

"All right," said his wife, "but you'll have to get some Lifesavers for me to throw."

* * *

Psychiatrist: Why do you say your wife treats you like a dog?

Exec: Well, for one thing, every time I get into bed with her, she rolls over and plays dead!

* * *

"Harriet is married to the chairman of a communications corporation."

"Bet she's not hurting for anything."

"She despises him."

"Really?"

"Harriet hates him so much she closes her eyes during intercourse so she doesn't have to see him enjoying himself."

* * *

Lipstick is a lovely gift
Every corporate wife reports,
Unless her hubby brings it home
On the front of his undershorts.

* * *

Did you hear about the electronics firm V.P. who took a mistress just to break the monogamy?

* * *

A suspicious Los Angeles auto dealer decided finally to have it out with his wife. He bought a gun and went home.

He silently unlocked the door and tiptoed into the bedroom. Just as he suspected, his wife was in bed making love with some strange guy.

"Okay," he said, pointing the pistol at the guy, "You're going to get it now!"

"Please, Nick," pleaded his wife, "don't kill him until he shows you how to do it."

* * *

Did you hear about the CEO who got to first base with the chorus girl, but was thrown out at home?

* * *

Harvey complained to his wife, "In our thirty-five years of marriage, we haven't been able to agree on anything."

"It's been thirty-six years," she retorted.

* * *

A postman was going to retire after thirty years service. His old-time customers knew about his leaving. The final morning, he knocked on Mrs. Bates's door. She was gorgeous and she invited him in. "Congratulations on your retirement. Let me fix you some breakfast," she said.

She fixed him ham, sausage, eggs, everything. Afterward, she took him up to her bedroom and made love to him. He had a wonderful time, and afterward she gave the postman two dollars.

"My goodness," he said, "what a terrific send-off you're giving me! But why the two dollars?"

"Well," she said, "it was really my husband's idea. This morning I mentioned that you were about to retire after 30 years, and I said, 'Isn't there something special we could do for him?' 'Screw him,' he said, 'give him two dollars.' . . . The breakfast was *my* idea."

* * *

Hubbard, a motion picture exec, came home sporting a pair of shoes he bought in Beverly Hills for $250 that day, He had anticipated admiring comments from his wife, but she didn't even appear to notice that he had them on.

Somewhat piqued, Hubbard waited until she was in bed and then marched into the bedroom stark naked, except for the fancy footwear.

He struck a pose and exclaimed, "It's about time you paid some attention to what my peter is pointing at!"

Looking down at the shoes, she muttered, "Too bad you didn't buy a hat."

LOVE
STOR

Husband: Did I hurt you?
Wife: No, why?
Husband: You moved!

* * *

Walker arrived home unexpectedly and found his wife naked on the suspiciously rumpled bed. A big, black cigar was burning in an ashtray. Since he did not smoke, Walker barked, where did that cigar come from?"

A naked man opened the closet door and said, "Havana!"

* * *

Hayward came home exhausted and terribly upset. "I was late for work today," he said to his wife.

"I know," she replied.

"I quarrelled with the boss."

"I know."

"He fired me," he said glumly.

"I know," she answered.

"How the hell do you know?"

"He told me."

"Ah, screw 'em!"

"I did," said his wife. "You go back to work on Monday."

* * *

Freida, a pretty, young blonde, started work as housekeeper at the Boyd house. The next day, while bending over, Freida's hair fell off. She was completely bald. "I'm sorry," she said to Mrs. Boyd, "I do not haf a single hair on my body."

"Don't worry about it," said her mistress.

That night when she told her husband, he got all excited. "I've always wondered what a woman looked like with no hair down *there!*" he cried. "Please, honey, get her down to the cellar tomorrow afternoon at five. I'll hide behind the storage boxes, and you try to talk her into showing you herself naked."

Mrs. Boyd agreed. Next day at 5 P.M. in the basement, she convinced Freida to remove her clothes so she could see what it was like for a girl to be without a single hair. Then Freida said, "Ma'am, I haf never saw one with hair on it, so you, too, should strip down!"

Mrs. Boyd did. Later at dinner she said to her husband, "I hope you're satisfied, because I was pretty embarrassed when she asked to see *mine*!"

"You were embarrassed?" shouted Boyd. "How do you think I felt? I had eight guys from the office hiding behind the boxes with me!"

* * *

Ellen and Sally were exchanging confidential secrets. "Last week I caught my husband with his secretary. She was taking a lot more than notes," said Ellen. "To punish the rat, I made him buy me a new dress."

"Did you also have him fire the girl?" asked Sally.

"No, not yet," replied Ellen. "I still need a hat and gloves."

* * *

Boss Boffs

The boss of a big Chicago firm was bawling out a salesman. The boss said, "Falkner, I understand that you were seen entertaining a prospective customer at the Palmer House last night, and enjoying an evening with your contact, at the firm's expense?"

"Ah, yes, I think I'm on to something there," he nodded.

"Could be," said the chief, "but one thing puzzles me. What would a girl who works in a massage parlor want with one of our wide-wheelbase, triple-track, heavy-duty 12-ton tractors?"

* * *

A person who is late when you're early and early when you're late.

* * *

Boss: You're late again; why?
Clerk: Sorry, I overslept.
Boss: What? Do you sleep at home, too?

* * *

The owner of a restaurant chain was talking to a friend in the health-club steam room. "I'm gonna have to fire my secretary."

"You mean the redhead with the big boobs?"

"Yeah. She's always interrupting my dictation and asking me to spell the simplest words—and it's embarrassing to have to keep saying, 'I don't know.' "

* * *

The sales manager said to his boss, "I wish I could afford a lovely, white fifty-six-foot ocean-going yacht like yours."

And his boss said, "So do I."

* * *

When the body was first made, all parts wanted to be boss.

The brain said, "Since I control everything and do all the thinking, I should be boss."

The feet said, "Since I carry man where he wants to go and get into positions to do what the brain wants, I should be boss."

The eyes said, "Since I must look out for all of you and tell you where the danger lurks, I should be boss."

And so it went with the heart, the ears, the lungs, and finally the asshole spoke up and demanded it be made boss.

All of the other parts laughed and laughed at the idea of an asshole being made boss. The asshole was so angered that he blocked himself off and refused to function. Soon, the brain was feverish, the eyes were crossed and ached, the feet were too weak to walk, the hands hung limply at the sides, and the heart and lungs struggled to keep going.

All pleaded with the brain to relent and let the asshole be boss. And so it happened. All the other parts did all the work and the asshole just bossed and passed out a lot of shit.

MORAL: You don't have to be a brain to be boss, just an asshole!

* * *

The boss's wife appeared unexpectedly in his office, and discovered her husband eating lunch—with his pretty secretary on his lap.

"Well," snorted the wife. "Explain this one, you worm!"

"Control yourself, dear," said her husband calmly. "You see all this food on the desk? I had to do something. The waiter forgot to send up a napkin."

Boss: If you work for us you'll have Christmas bonus, profit sharing, complete health and dental coverage, an expense account, a company car, stock options, and a subsidized mortgage.

Yuppie: Fine, but what d'you pay?

Boss: Surely you don't expect a salary as well!

* * *

"Your new secretary is very attractive."
"Yes, and she's trisexual."
"Trisexual? What does that mean?"
"She'll try anything!"

* * *

Did you hear about the manufacturer who accumulated millions making men's suits, and lost it all making a skirt?

* * *

A worker asked his boss for a raise. "After all, I'm doing the work of three men," he said.

"Tell me who the other two are," said his employer, "and I'll fire them."

* * *

Winkelman, a big manufacturer of ladies' lingerie in New York, received word that his top traveling salesman had died of a heart attack in a Phoenix hotel.

Winkelman sent this telegram collect:

RETURN SAMPLES BY FREIGHT AND SEARCH HIS PANTS FOR ORDERS.

* * *

Grossman, a wealthy textile manufacturer visiting Las Vegas, offered to give a hundred dollars to spank Karen, a chorus girl, on her bare behind. A friend who knew the girl arranged matters with her and all three went up to Karen's apartment.

She lay down on the bed with her dress up and Grossman began caressing her buttocks, marveling at their warmth, sliding his fingers in and out of her honeypot.

"Go ahead, hit her!" urged the friend. "What are you waiting for?"

"Why should I?" said Grossman. "This feels wonderful and it's not costing me a dime."

* * *

"To get ahead in the business world," said Alma to her friend, "you gotta get under a good man and work up."

* * *

"How's Felicia making out in her new job?"

"Well, she was such a wonderful secretary that the boss made her a partner. Then she stayed late one night and he gave her the business."

* * *

Lefkowitz, the dress manufacturer, kept a goldfish in a bowl on his desk. One day his sales manager noticed it. "What's that for?"

"It's nice," replied Lefkowitz, "to have something around that opens his mouth without asking for a raise."

* * *

Shoenfeld and Dubin were discussing their bosses. "My boss," said Shoenfeld, "is such a cheapskate, he should only drop dead!"

"My boss is different," smiled Dubin. "You just can't help liking him. 'Cause if you don't he fires you!"

* * *

"How'd you find your secretary, Harry?"

"I saw this want ad: *Secretary wants job—no bad habits—willing to learn*. So I hired her."

* * *

Weinstein called in his director of sales. When he had settled comfortably in a chair, the boss said, "I've been looking through your sales record for the month. What makes you think we're a non-profit organization?"

* * *

The police were investigating the death of Markowitz, the dress manufacturer, who had jumped from a window of his office. The detective decided to query Marlene, his lovely, young secretary.

"Can you offer any explanation?" he asked the girl.

"Well, after working for Mr. Markowitz one month," she began, "I got a forty-dollar a week raise. At the end of the second month he gave me a beautiful black negligee.

"At the end of the third month he gave me a new Thunderbird and a stunning Persian lamb coat. Then he asked me if I'd be willing to make love to him and how much would I charge him.

"I told him, because he'd been so nice to me, I'd charge him only ten dollars—even though I was getting twenty from the other guys in the office. And that's when he jumped out the window!"

* * *

The boss's wife dropped in at his office and found him squatting on his haunches, taking a book from the bottom shelf. Quickly, she ripped off her clothes, tiptoed up behind him, wrapped her legs around his shoulders, dangled her bare boobs over his eyes, and asked, "Guess who?"

Her husband groaned, "Get back to your typewriter, Miss Gonzalez. You know it's not time for the coffee break yet!"

BIG DEALS

CAREER WOMAN

One who would rather go out
and take orders than stay
home and be boss.

* * *

"I'm sorry you'll have to leave us," said the boss, "but it may cheer you to learn that it's costing us $200,000 to get a computer in your place."

* * *

Joy, while working late one night
Turned out every office light.
Her boss beside her whispered things,
Of wedding bells and diamond rings.
He pledged his love in burning phrase
And acted foolish forty ways.
When he had gone Joy gave a laugh
And then turned off the dictograph.

* * *

Andrea was complaining to her boyfriend about the unhappy circumstances at the office.

"That boss of yours must be a real prick," he said sympathetically.

"Not really," said the girl. "He's such a phony I prefer to classify him as a dildo."

* * *

Mrs. Rappaport advertised a new Cadillac for fifty dollars.

Finley answered the ad and the first thing he asked was, "What's wrong with the car?"

"Nothing," she replied. "If you want it for fifty dollars give me the money and take it away. If you don't want it, please don't waste my time."

Finley asked for the keys and went to the garage. He backed the car out, parked in front of the house, counted out fifty dollars, and handed it to the owner.

"Now you have your money, what's the catch?"

"My husband just died," she said, "and in his will he instructed that the Cadillac be sold and the proceeds be given his secretary."

* * *

An economics graduate was offered the chance of a lifetime as personal assistant to a financier. Eagerly he asked the terms.

Financier: You receive $30,000 a year for making every worry of mine your own.

Graduate: Fine, but where's the $30,000 coming from?

Financier: That's your first worry.

* * *

A group of men gave a testimonial dinner to Fleigelman and, after praising him for an hour, the honoree finally got up to speak. "Gentlemen," he said, "when I came to this town forty-one years ago, I walked down a dirt road with one suit of clothes one pair of shoes, carrying a stick with a red handkerchief tied to the end of it. And to show you what hard work can do along with the great opportunities this country can offer, today I own three banks, five apartment houses, and ten oil wells!"

Everybody applauded, and right after the dinner one salesman walked up to the old man saying, "Pardon me, sir, I'd like to ask you a question. When you came here forty-one years ago with just that one suit, a pair of shoes, and the stick with a red handkerchief tied to it—what was in the handkerchief?"

The old man said, "I had three million dollars in bonds and two hundred thousand dollars in cash!"

* * *

"My boss keeps drumming his fingers all the time I'm in his office," said the secretary, "and it's beginning to bother me."

"Can't you just ignore it?" her roommate inquired.

"Oh, I suppose I could—except for the fact that it's murder on my panty hose!"

The boss's relatives.

* * *

A Detroit bartender had been keeping not only his tips but half the house receipts as well. If he was given four dollars, automatically two dollars went into his own pocket. This went on for six months. One night a man handed the bartender a five dollar bill and he put it all in his pocket. The boss noticed it, tapped him on the shoulder, and said, "What'sa matter, Joe, ain't we partners no more?"

* * *

Noticing that her boss's fly was open, the embarrassed secretary told him as she left the office, "Your garage door is open."

The bewildered exec didn't know what she meant until a co-worker finally told him what she was referring to. The next day, he called his secretary into his office and said, "Yesterday, when my garage door was open, did you see a long red Cadillac with a hard top?"

"Oh, no," she replied. "It was a little pink Volkswagen with two flat tires up front."

* * *

"Why did that pretty new steno get fired?"

"She objected to taking down everything the boss wanted her to."

* * *

Visitor: Is the boss busy with his secretary?

Receptionist: Yeah, he's up to her knees in work!

* * *

WILDE ON WILDE

I love humor. I've spent over thirty years studying, analyzing, researching, teaching, performing, and writing it. The fascination started in Jersey City where I was born in 1928. As a kid during the Depression I had to scratch hard to make a buck, and making jokes was a way of life.

After a two-year stint in the Marine Corps, where I found I could make leathernecks laugh, I worked my way through the University of Miami in Florida, doing a comedy act at the hotels. After graduating, I entertained in night clubs and theaters around the U.S. I got to play Vegas and Tahoe and the other big-time spots being the "supporting" comedian for Ann-Margret, Debbie Reynolds, Pat Boone, and many others.

I've done acting roles on *Mary Tyler Moore*, *Rhoda*, *Sanford & Son* and other sitcoms; performed on Carson, Griffin and Douglas, and I've done a bunch of TV commercials.

This is my 35th joke book. I'm also proud of the two serious works I've done on comedy technique: *The Great Comedians Talk About Comedy* and *How the Great Comedy Writers Create Laughter*. Both books have been called "definitive" works on the subject.

My books have sold over 8,000,000 copies, which makes them the best-selling humor series in publishing history. And while I'm blowing my own horn here, the best thing I ever did was to marry Maryruth Poulos, a beautiful and talented writer from Wyoming.

Other Books by Larry Wilde

The Official Bedroom/Bathroom Joke Book
More The Official Smart Kids/Dumb Parents Joke Book
The Official Book of Sick Jokes
More The Official Jewish/Irish Joke Book
The Last Official Italian Joke Book
The Official Cat Lovers/Dog Lovers Joke Book
The Official Dirty Joke Book
The *Last* Official Polish Joke Book
The Official Golfers Joke Book
The Official Smart Kids/Dumb Parents Joke Book
The Official Religious/Not So Religious Joke Book
More The Official Polish/Italian Joke Book
The Official Black Folks/White Folks Joke Book
The Official Virgins/Sex Maniacs Joke Book
The Official Jewish/Irish Joke Book
The Official Polish/Italian Joke Book

In hardcover

THE COMPLETE BOOK OF ETHNIC HUMOR
HOW THE GREAT COMEDY WRITERS CREATE LAUGHTER
THE GREAT COMEDIANS TALK ABOUT COMEDY